CINDERELLA'S FAMILY
A Feminist View of Family and Matriarchy
From Primate to 22nd Century Family
B. P. Meinhardt

October 27, 2014; 3.1416 Publishing, doc1644@gmail.com

Other books of interest:

The AFGHAN QUEEN
American Business Woman and her 5 Years in Afghanistan
http://www.afghanqueen.net/

MOM SAVES THE UNIVERSE
Cosmic Energy/World Peace/Reaching the Stars/Matriarch Rule/Future Reality Novel
http://www.amazon.com/MOM-SAVES-THE-UNIVERSE-Feminist-ebook/dp/B00MJKVYCM

MOTHER: EARTH/ENERGY/COSMOS
Erotic Energy and the Cosmic Family
http://www.amazon.com/MOTHER-EARTH-ENERGY-COSMOS-Matriarchs-ebook/dp/B00LR37SLI

CINDERELLA'S HOUSEWORK,
Families in Crises, Households at the Edge of Chaos
http://www.cinderellashousework.net/194391777

ISBN-13: 978-1503002760
ISBN-10: 1503002764

CINDERELLA'S FAMILY

Contents

Contents	2
1-Introduction, pic 1	3
2-Cinderella's Labor, pics 2-4	6
3-Housework-Wagework, pics 5-6	12
4-Labor Pains, pics 7-11	16
5-Housework Production, pics 12-16	30
6-Housework Profit, pics 17-20	41
7-Productive Consumption, pics 21-23	50
8-Wealth of Nations, pics 24-26	53
9-Birth of Property, pics 27-39	58
10-Haves and Have-nots, pics 40-47	69
11-Our only home is *change*, pics 48-63	81
12-Household Religion, pics 64-83	91
13-Abundance and Scarcity, pics 84-87	113
14-Lysistrata, pics 88-91	122
15-What's to be done? pics 92-95	128
16-Do we have a future? pics 96-108	139
17-Year 2090, pics 109-114	167
18-Energy Futures, pics 115-122	181
19-Year 2100, pics 123-129	191
20-How to boil a frog	199
21-Visual sources, pic 130	201

1-Introduction: *Cinderella's Family* was planned as a doctoral thesis about the global economics of family and housework. This book broadens and updates the original.

This book examines housework, focusing on the social-economy of the global family. *Cinderella's Family* is a cross-cultural synthesis emphasizing the role of the family in the on-going global economic crisis.

Cinderella portrays family oppression. *Cinderella* remains a powerful symbol of household drudgery, as well as a popular children's story. It is also a tale of family transformation. *Cinderella* suggests the origins of the nuclear family. The degradation and isolation of the nuclear family is a consequence of globalizing the profit-economy.

Over the last 2,500 years, patriarchs treated families as commodities. Families are consumers, houseworkers, wageworkers, and sex-workers. Economic need forces people to *choose* life as a *commodity*, to be bought and sold like potatoes. It amounts to coerced servitude in an increasingly sociopath global profit-economy.

Radical contradictions in society are a prelude to upheaval. Consider the vast global imbalance of wealth. Super-wealthy *Haves* take possession of the world. They are *Takers*, taking what they want, and devouring the Earth in the process of possessing it.

1-Venus of Laussel, Dordogne, France 40,000 BC
http://en.wikipedia.org/wiki/Venus_of_Laussel

Daniel Quinn, in *The Story of B, An Adventure of the Mind and Spirit,* uses the analogy of a slowly heating cauldron of humanity. Paleontologists, Anthropologists, Archeologists, and Geologists amass data indicating humanity is three-million years old.

Cataclysmic *die-offs* decimated life on Earth numerous times. The last *die-off* occurred 15,000 years ago, ending in a rapid global warming cycle, polar ice retreat, tectonic plate shifts, and global tsunamis. Human survivors were limited to thousands, in contrast to the pre-flood millions.

Jericho is 12,000 years old, an early grain cultivation site. Large scale agriculture is evidenced 10,000 years ago at Çatalhöyük in Anatolia, Turkey. http://en.wikipedia.org/wiki/Jericho & http://en.wikipedia.org/wiki/%C3%87atalh%C3%B6y%C3%BCk

The *Genesis* story of Cain the farmer and Abel the herdsman is a parable about *Takers* and *Leavers,* dating back thousands of years before the *Bible* was written.

4

As in the American West of the 1800s, farmers and herders were continually at each-others' throats. They fought mostly over access to land and water.

The cauldron of humanity has slowly warmed over the last 10,000 years. Farmer Cain and herder Abel fought. Both were *Takers* attempting to expand their holdings.

2-Astarte represents the nature fertility in early Europe
Louvre Museum http://en.wikipedia.org/wiki/Astarte

The Cain-Abel conflict is a story of patriarch *Taker* mentality. For 10,000 years *Takers* have advanced the belief that the world exists for their taking. Competitors are either absorbed into *Taker* culture or destroyed.

Taker culture depends on *Totalitarian agriculture, belief* in global expansion as a *God-given right. Taker* belief includes the *Great Forgetting* of 3-million years of matriarch stability. *Leavers* are tribal hunter-gatherers, content with stability and without thought of consuming the world. *Takers* set the global cauldron boiling.

Graphics throughout this book depict aspects of the household throughout antiquity. As seen in the graphics of Astarte with lions, cats and people follow the evolutionary survival trail together.

2-Cinderella's Labor: *The Poor child was given all the rough housework to do.* (Charles Perrault, *Cinderella*, 1697)
Perrault's other books had already appeared for children: *Red Riding Hood* and *Tales of Mother Goose. Jack and the Beanstalk, The Pied Piper, Beauty and the Beast*, and *Dick Wittington and His Cat* were other popular children's books. These entertained and instructed children about the virtues of merchant society.

Cinderella is a parable of merchant society. It is also a story of the nuclear family and the form of housework that develops in the nuclear family of parents and children.

Her father's remarriage and the selfish vanity of the step-family make *Cinderella* the victim of housework. The death her mother together with her father's remarriage creates the basis of *Cinderella's* abuse.

Cinderella works *inside* so the step-family can pursue life *outside*. Family income depends on the father's trade outside the home. The story is more a forecast and less a fairy tale. The exploited servant is replaced by the oppressed houseworker of today.

6

3-Athens Astarte with animals and solar symbols, 650 BC

The source of the conflict is the transition from the old tribal cottage-craft to the new market society. It is a change from matriarchal *Leavers* to patriarchal *Takers*.

Cinderella represents the household as the totality of society, while the step-family represents the fragmentation of the household. In the old society, the tribal household was the totality of all social-economic activities. All work and social life occurred within the enveloping warmth of the stabile matriarch tribal family.

Cinderella's fate is similar to that of the old tribal household. In merchant society, houseworker status declines while work status outside the home increases.

The advent of the nuclear family meant that fewer people were left at home to do the housework. *Cinderella's* fate is similar to that of most houseworkers. Their value as people declines to the extent they are trapped by housework.

Cinderella's step-sisters represent the transition from a mother oriented tribal household to a father dominated nuclear family. The step-family aspired to social position in the new market society. The impetus of the new patriarchal structure of post-feudal Europe depended on close political-economic alliances between local princes and merchants.

The culture required prominent merchant families attend state functions. Thus, *Cinderella* and step-family were invited to the prince's ball.

The Great Escape: Cinderella's message is: 'old tribal society was more humane; but we are stuck with the new market society, and its dehumanizing effects, so we might as well make the best of it. We can't change it, but as individuals we might escape.'

The adventurous can escape the nuclear family prison. That is why *Cinderella* and her step-sisters are desperate to go to the ball. It's their chance to escape.

The problem today as it was 300 years ago is that too many people need to escape; but there is no prince to rescue us. Strangest of all is how *Cinderella* escapes.

In the age of mercantilism, money and reason meant the same thing. *Cinderella* is something of an innovator as she uses neither money nor reason to solve her problem. She resorts to the power of the old Nature religion.

Perhaps the major contradiction faced by *Cinderella* was the nature of housework. She was caught in the crunch of underdevelopment: the endless repetition of housework drudgery. Most oppressive is the drag of daily housework leaving no clear-cut break between tasks. *Cinderella* was aware that housework was destroying her chance to grow. *Cinderella*'s future depended on the old Hearth religion.

The fairy godmother shows the fairytale origin of the story. Most children's stories are rooted in folk tales and mythology. Tribal society is linked with Hearth religion, with its focus on *fertility,* hearth power, and mothers.

The Power: *Cinderella's* fairy godmother is Hestia of the hearth. The godmother is the spirit of household fertility, holding transformative power over nature.

The fairy godmother is the Great Goddess, Good Woman, Great Mother, Wise Woman, and Hestia of the hearth. For the young she is referred to as *Mother Goose*. Her rhymes are incantations, invoking the power of Mother-Nature.

Great Mother controls all life, as well as the elements of life and death; just as the family mother controls family life. These powers reside in the household and mother's command of life's elements: Earth, Air, Fire, and Water.

When *Cinderella* called her godmother she also called the Old Religion to escape family oppression. Her godmother instructed her to fetch the largest pumpkin and the rats from the traps. Rather than be surprised by these directions, *Cinderella* clearly knew what must be done.

Cinderella, with godmother help, took control of her household power. With hearth magic, *Cinderella* renewed her power over life and finally discovered her own power.

Her return to Nature religion symbolizes her recognition that all power is in her hands as she controls the household creative forces. The ultimate power of mothers is they control fertility, to bear children or not. This is the most powerful magic.

With godmother's help *Cinderella* uses her power to transform pumpkins into coaches and rats into footmen. She makes the ultimate discovery: women control the elemental power of life to produce people.

Out of the Broom Closet: *Cinderella's* confinement to housework was the result of the new market economy. The new life of father and step-family *outside* the household only existed because of *Cinderella's* work *within* the home.

Cinderella represents the confrontation between housework and work outside the home. The struggle pits production for family against production for profit.

The communal need of family is confronted by the self-serving interest of the market. In this way family labor becomes an unpaid market commodity. *Cinderella* is more a social casualty than a hero. Her isolation, while an individual tragedy, is more the result of a new form of household, the nuclear family. If she was isolated in the household it was because the home had newly become an isolating institution. The story reflects the coercion of market society.

Summary: What is seen in the *Cinderella* story is a tale of conflicts of middle class family life in 17th Century mercantile Europe. These conflicts were so severe that permanent struggle arose between work inside and outside the home. *Cinderella* embodies these conflicts. We can decipher from the story a peculiar struggle:

1) Family life *inside* the household is challenged by social life *outside*;

2) Household family *crafts* are confronted with *commodity* production for the market place;

3) As *wagework* becomes more productive, *housework* becomes less so;

4) Conflict between *matriarch* tribal family and *patriarch* nuclear family becomes institutionalized;

5) The household takes on the opposite attributes of the market place. Households become isolating, imprisoning

house workers, and perpetuating the under-development of house workers;

6) Housework is deprived of its craft value degenerating into a chaos of divisive tasks, each expanding to fill the available hours in the day.

4-Astarte Crete fertility mother with lions, pottery shard 635 BC

With these ideas in mind, the following chapters provide an analysis of family and housework. The overall purpose of this book involves far more than an economic examination. *Cinderella* chapters focus on the cross-cultural challenges at the core of family, household, and human life.

3-Housework-Wagework: Housework is the vital link for all social-economic activities. The *Cinderella* story models this connection. Examining this process, one sees it as a vast mix of conflicts between work *inside* and *outside* the home. As wageworkers and houseworkers, we are involved in the care of family, even if it's one person living alone.

A conflict arises because the activities of the household involve caring for *people*, while wagework involves the production of *things*. Housework is a natural process. While wagework produces commodities and services, housework *produces people producing everything else*.

Both wagework and housework reflect the peculiar attitudes of the market economy. Since both are forms of labor, they both suffer the side effects of being dreary, stupefying, repetitious, and dehumanizing.

Numerous studies examined both housework and wagework. Both cause anxiety, self-hatred, and self-shame. Eventually, impulses such as these are manifest as a desperate need for change, either inward causing self-destruction or outward in the form of radical action.

Tools: To a large extent housework is shaped by household tools. These often have a fragmenting, disorganizing, and *make-work* effect. On the other hand wagework goes to the opposite extreme with over-regimentation. Both extremes cause conflict in the work place and the home.

Rather than being productive tools, the tools of the household and factory seem more designed to impose control than to get the job done. There is a public character to wagework lacking in housework.

Wagework requires people be brought together under the same roof, providing an important opportunity for working people to socialize. In contrast, houseworkers are faced with daily isolation and loneliness.

The euphemism is 'household privacy.' We are born into a *private* family, while living in a *public* world. Where is our first loyalty? We build loyalties to people on the job; but family comes first.

The *public* world of wagework conflicts with the *private* world of housework. The more deeply we are involved in housework, the poorer the chance for a life outside the home. This was Cinderella's discovery.

Teamwork results in things made by people working together in the workplace. On the other hand, the *isolation* of a houseworker hides the work in plain sight. Caring for ourselves and bearing children is the most important work of all. It is *producing people,* the basis of all production.

Isolation: Profit system media promote bogus freedom; while workplace teamwork is transformed into isolated servitude for most houseworkers.

5-Thisbe Astarte with Swans, Earth Mother 660 BC

Privacy and *individualism* are new fetishes, replacing cooperation. The profit-economy creates household isolation; but requires teamwork on the job.

People are nurtured in the home. Households create people and humanity. The household is the origin of our humanity; but also the source of human conflict. Conflicts are created in the home because that's where people are nurtured and socialized. The conflict between work *inside* and *outside* the home has the same source.

Heart of the struggle: There is a basic contradiction between housework and wagework. The struggle for *equality* causes a reappraisal of income *inequality*. Can we have human equality without income equality?

By challenging inequality in the courts, the struggle unifies theory and practice. It's part of the income struggle. Most significant, the struggle links ideas and actions.

Profit-culture blunders on with its *Taker* mentality, expanding on Earth and into outer space. The defeat of American expansion in South-East Asia is usually analyzed from the viewpoint of hardware, troop numbers, kills, firepower, and population control. It's a *body count* mentality, a dehumanization of people. Similarly, the Middle East wars prove to be interminable and inconclusive.

Looking at the external aspects of the *Cinderella* story reveals a woman's struggle against the cruelty of her step-family. A deeper view suggests a complex social-political

15

perspective. Only when internal and external aspects are examined can a more realistic picture emerge.

6-Mother-Child, Early Nativity Prototype, 300 AD

4-Labor Pains: *And while her step-sisters were surrounded with every comfort and luxury and lived a life of ease, the younger girl swept and dusted their rooms, washed dishes, scrubbed the floor and steps and worked from morning till night.* (Charles Perrault, *Cinderella,* 1697) What is the purpose of housework, and how is it different from other types of work? Apart from mating there's a more basic value to housework. People strive to live and prosper. People need: food, clothing, shelter, diversions, sex, kids, and comfort. This is housework.

Every type of work that involves caring for people is the domain of housework. Every task, from birth to death, to the extent work is needed, is part of housework. Caring for ourselves is housework. When others care for us they do housework. *Housework is real and vital work.*

Regardless of rationalization, housework is vital work since it produces our lives. ***Housework is productive as it produces people, the most important product of all.*** Since

16

human life is of primary importance, the household may be thought of as the most important of all *factories*, since family households produce people. Wagework does little more than provide family income. The same can be said of all goods and services existing to supply the needs and desires of families.

Housework is an evolutionary advance as people began working *consciously* to care for each other. Other critters perform similar functions *instinctively*. We depend on conscious awareness as well as basic instinct.

Housework images: We are challenged as housework must be performed *consciously*, rather than *instinctively*. The basic contradiction is the dehumanizing nature of *housework* inside the home compared to outside *wagework*.

Ann Oakley in her book *The Sociology of Housework* documented the dehumanizing nature of housework by means of a series of interviews with English women. http://en.wikipedia.org/wiki/Ann_Oakley *The Sociology of Housework.*

'Throughout the 40 interviews a clear perception of housework as work emerges. The women in the interviews experience and define housework as labor, akin to that demanded by any job.'

When 40 women were asked: 'What would you say are the *worst things about being a housewife*? Fourteen replied

17

housework; fourteen replied *monotony, repetitiousness, and boredom;* six said *constant domestic responsibility*; four said *Isolation and Loneliness*; three each replied *must get housework done; being tied down*; and two said *Children.*

Most women said the most gratifying aspect of housework is children. While the objective of housework is caring for and producing *people*; most other work outside the home is directed toward producing *things.*

Our humanity values *people* over *things*; yet the reality of the profit-system places a major value on *things*. This is a serious conflict as long as *property* is valued above *people.*

Cycles of *prosperity* and *crisis* persist as the profit-economy manipulates *demand* and *scarcity* for profit.
Increasingly, the profit-economy produces commodities by automation, while fabricating scarcity via low wages. Less income means less buying.

The 1,000 super-wealthy families fear that the other 2-billion families will become increasingly aware of the pyramid of wealth they support. The Internet is as much an information source as a cash cow, and increasingly a source of anger.

In terms of labor and production, *housework* and *wagework* have some basic elements in common. Both are productive; both use similar tools; and both depend on the mental and physical abilities of people.

Cinderella's household: The link between housework and wagework is revealed in the split between the two. *Cinderella* represents the split between housework and wagework. While she worked in the home, her father worked outside in the mercantile world. Both *Cinderella* and her father shared important functions.

7-**Astarte Arkadia,** Crete with plants and animals 1,000 BC

Cinderella produced people by performing housework. To the extent she cared for the family she *produced* it. Her housework was as specialized and important as her father's work. Her work depended on the planning skills necessary to perform an unbroken chain of routine and disconnected tasks. She needed intelligence to sustain her struggle within the deteriorating step-family.

Work as social: Wagework is different from housework. Gathering workers in teams create a social workplace. While income and employment are vital, there is also a basic need for work that maintains social contacts.

Workplace socialization contrasts sharply with household isolation. Ann Oakley's interviews with 40 housewives suggest: *isolation*, *loneliness*, and *boredom* contribute to housework dissatisfaction.

Children are often the focus of housework and the main source of satisfaction. In addition, coffee-klatch, gossip, and shopping often satisfy a similar social need, as do wage worker-teams. Talking to store clerks and other shoppers is often a high point of a lonely shopper's day.

Researchers have long recognized the value of improved job satisfaction, as well as workplace productivity, with opportunities for socialization, especially as work teams. Isolation eventually drives intelligent women to seek extreme forms of relief. In antiquity, relief was available in the form of Pelasgian Hearth religion.

8-Hestia Goddess of hearth, home, architecture, family, Domesticity, and the state, http://en.wikipedia.org/wiki/Hestia

Hestia of the Hearth is the ancient Pelasgian Goddess of hearth, home, and family. Unlike other deities, Hestia did not stray from home; but unlike Cinderella, Hestia held the power of family life and death. Hestia was honored in all social-political activities. She received the first and last wine libations of all festivals. Natural religion persists from ancient Mystery religion, and especially from Hestia of the Hearth, providing a spectrum of social-cultural life.

Dealing with the problem of household isolation *Cinderella* again provides a convenient model. She is the symbol of household *isolation*. Her *loneliness* and desperation to escape the prison of housework was evident in her desire to go to the prince's ball.

Cinderella turns to Natural religion. Escape from household drudgery is not easy. Extreme action is needed. She could be bartered-off for a *bride price* or appeal to her fairy godmother. Could she escape without her godmother?

Subversion of housework: There is a common tendency to demean housework. Perhaps housework is degraded because it is a cultural-economic threat to the market place.

If one considers that housework involves caring for and producing *loved ones* such as children, then it becomes clear why housework threatens the market system.

Wagework produces commodities in exchange for wages. Wageworkers lose control of what they produce as these products, once produced, become owners' property; but, housework is inalienable labor as the work done at home binds the family closely. Unlike family, wagework social bonds are easily broken by the employer.

The threat to wagework is that people would prefer to work for themselves and their family, given the choice. This is why in colonial America with unlimited land, few had to work for wages or be enslaved, if they were white men. Most whites could become homesteaders, self-sufficient farmers, herders, crafters, and householders. As anti-slave tactics, the various *Homestead acts* provided a ticket to economic liberation for masses of people.

Manufacturing was first *cottage crafts*. Perhaps this is why the *gray* market for moonshine and drugs continues to expand. http://en.wikipedia.org/wiki/Homestead_Acts

All such small-scale family enterprise is a threat to the profit-system. This is why household industry will always subvert the market economy. Regardless of the number of laws passed in their favor, super-rich *Haves* tend to fear home enterprise. *Haves* cannot exist without wagework. This is why they feverishly pursue automation, to reduce dependency on people.

Haves live in constant fear of *Have-nots,* as reducing wagework reduces income. With reduced income, *Have-nots* reduce purchases. *Haves* continue to cut wages and income, yet expect purchases to increase as well as profits.

The great contradiction is: *Haves* can't teach robots to buy the products that robots produce. *Haves* live in a

self-imposed paradox. *Haves* **can produce without wageworkers, but not without wageworker purchases.**

The relationship between Cinderella and her step-family illustrates this situation. Cinderella *spent* herself in the daily drudgery of step-family housework. As she cared for them, she *produced* them and produced her own *underdevelopment.*

In return, the step-family heaped abuse on her and degraded her effort. The step-family realized that Cinderella's work was essential to maintain their social status. The leisure time for step-family social pursuits was made possible by Cinderella's labor.

The abuse was the result of a contradiction posed by the need for Cinderella's housework and the potential loss of such service jeopardizing step-family social aspirations. One might imagine Cinderella represents housework and the step-family represents the emerging mercantile system.

Hostility increases as family and marketplace are aware of their dependency on those who work and purchase.

Cinderella dramatizes the subversion of households. By isolating the household from society, *Haves* initiate the degradation of household *Have-nots.*

9-Boetia Astarte with geese and sun signs 750 BC

Fabricating artificial inequalities between people, *Haves* wage an interminable war against *Have-nots*.

Housework inalienable labor: Why is housework a threat to the market system? We know that the work we do for our family is inalienable, as it is work we do for the people we love. As we produce our family we produce ourselves and strengthen bonds of loving affection.

Working for the *Haves* there is always the thought *'why work for them when we can work for our family?'* *Haves* are bosses. *Have-nots* are wageworkers and houseworkers.

Why do *Have-nots* work for wages? Wage workers must work for wages to provide income to support their family. If other options were available most wage workers would choose other ways to support their family. Home-brew supported families for centuries and continue to do so.

After the decline of Feudalism and prior to the Industrial revolution, clan, tribe, cooperative, and commune were viable options. These options persist in homesteading, crafts, and in the *underground economy*.

24

To protect profits, it is in the interest of *Haves* to break family and kinship bonds. As there is always a tendency for wage workers to favor family over employer, the profits of the *Haves* benefit from the break-up of *Have-not* families.

Family division is evident in the growing proportion of single parent and especially single mother families.
One need only study government statistics of families to see the reality of family division. In 2014 less than half of U.S. families included a married couple.

Dehumanizing housework: To increase the wealth of the *Haves*, *Have-nots* are degraded by reduced income. All workers suffer from income cuts. High pay full-time jobs are split into low-pay part-time work. This trend continues since the 1980s, with the break-up of the phone monopoly.

Haves profess to support abstract *family values*. Actual *Have* family values amount to *cutting income*. Sociopath values reduce families to stressed-out workers and consumers, with less income to spend. *Have family values* send the global economy spiraling downward, as income is reduced. Families, especially single parent families, suffer monotony, housework fragmentation, and loneliness. Hopelessness develops as opportunities for income, self-development, and status evaporate.

Since housework does not lend itself to factory control or disciplined routine, the masters of the market place consider housework the weak link in the profit-system. *Direct* control of the family is too costly; therefore *indirect* control via biased education and media lowers family expectations.

10-Maia Astarte with goose and fox 600 BC

Illusions of freedom: Media coerces people into buying junk gadgets, rather than useful tools. These are designed as: items for *consumption* rather than production. These tend to be easily broken, replaced, and *superfluous*.

Gadgets are costly, low quality, entrapping, and make extra work; extending work to fill the available hours. Yet it is precisely the household environment that requires the most skillful organization and planning.

One need only consider housework functions to realize a houseworker must be: lover, teacher, mother, father, doctor, nurse, entertainer, laborer, cook, gardener, care-giver, janitor, purchasing agent, psychologist, protector, moralist, judge, jury, planner, organizer, and chauffer.

Most important, houseworkers must be humble servants. Why is housework considered unproductive and trivial? Housework is trivialized as *Haves* own the media.

Housework produces people! What's unproductive and trivial about that? Paddy Quick's *Women's Work* notes:
'The illusion of an unproductive houseworker results from the many small essentially unimportant bits of work during the day. The work continues as long as there is work to do.'
http://www.tandfonline.com/doi/abs/10.1080/07393148008429505?journalCode=cnps20 #.U-9FPmd0wfo

The highest level of skill and intelligence receives no tangible reward and this is becoming a major problem. It's a system of unpaid labor and indoctrinated values, backed by force. At the same time the package of *Have family values* is cloaked in fantasy sentimentalities.

Tribal and nuclear family housework: Tribal societies existed from the earliest period of antiquity. Today they persist at the periphery of market society. Tribal societies share among hundreds. This contrasts sharply with the nuclear family sharing among a few.

The nuclear family household seldom consists of more than three people, the statistical average. The classic nuclear family model, with married couple and kids, is now more likely to consist of an unmarried couple, a single parent and child, or one person.

In tribal society there is little distinction between housework and other forms of work. Development of tribal culture tends to be less specialized compared to the highly specialized and divided nuclear family. Tribal groups tend to treat all activities as an integrated social unity of work, play, ritual, culture, and all aspects of life.

Tribal and market societies contrast sharply. Comparing the nuclear family to a tribal group such as the Mbuti forest pygmies in the Democratic Republic of the Congo reveal sharp differences. http://en.wikipedia.org/wiki/Mbuti_people

While Ituri Forest Mbuti lives as unified families in bands of 15 to 60 people, they are essentially a hunter-gatherer society. Mbuti society is rooted in the Ituri forest.

Researchers often study unique groups of people noting factors such as: 1) social-economic structure, 2) division of work, 3) sex-labor distinctions, 4) tool use and ownership, 5) area of work domination, 6) social ownership, 7) form of marriage, 8) value system, 9) culture development, and 10) overall societal objectives. Typically, tribes place more importance on *people* than *things*.

In contrast to the profit economy, Mbuti live by daily communal food gathering. The well-stocked Ituri rain forest is so abundant that only a few hours of daily gathering are needed to supply most needs. Mbuti women and men share hunting, gathering, food preparation, and even child care. Although women and men have different hunting tasks, they both participate.

On the other hand, market society requires 99.8% of *Have-not* families devote their time and attention to wagework, housework, and generating income for themselves, and super-profits for the 0. 2% of *Haves*.

11-Sparta Astarte with ravens, 650 BC

Almost as soon as they can walk, children, women, and men are self-sufficient food gatherers. Two-thirds of Mbuti food is *gathered*; while only one-third is *hunted*.

The independence provided by food gathering contributes to Mbuti equality as well as exceptionally good health. Mbuti accept virtually all sexual variation as normal. Except for some comic ridicule, even incest is tolerated. Tolerance seems greater in societies with shared affluence.

The point to be made is that the division of household labor is largely the result of social-economic patterns and may ultimately depend on environment. Specifically, living in the Ituri Forest provides an *affluent* environment.

29

Family formation is neither natural nor instinctive. Rather it's learned and embedded in society over long periods. Three million years of human society evolve as: bands, hordes, clans, tribes, families, and communes. A natural or fabricated *affluent* society tends to favor unspecialized, communal, egalitarian, and low stress life styles.

This is seen in rain-forest, South Pacific, Amazon, Northwest Pacific Coast, Hutterite communes, and other cultures outside the market economy.

5-HOUSEWORK PRODUCTION: *In the evening when her work was done the poor girl would sit in the chimney corner among the ashes and embers for warmth and because of this she was called Cinderella.* (Charles Perrault, *Cinderella*, 1697)

Housework is productive. As did Cinderella, we feed, clothe, clean, and care for ourselves and others. Even if a person lives alone, similar labor constitutes housework. **We produce people thru the process of housework.**

Officials do not consider housework a productive activity. Housework is omitted from the Gross Domestic Product, GDP.

Few economists recognize housework as productive. GDP is the sum of consumption, investment, government spending, and exports. But housework is excluded from GDP. http://en.wikipedia.org/wiki/Gross_Domestic_Product_(GDP).

Consumption includes all goods and services produced. GDP totals final *household consumption-expenditure;* but not the work needed to convert consumption into people.

GDP includes all *wage-income* and *consumption,* as well as all tools of production. Household tools are included in GDP, but not housework. What's missing from the GDP?

Everything produced is included in the GDP, except housework that produces *People.* Housework producing people is hashed into the great remainders-bin of *Externalities*—swept under the economic rug. *Externalities* are *Non-market transactions,* such as *household production* and volunteer or *unpaid services.*

Houseworkers shop, buy, and consume. Are these not *market transactions*? The family household is a flesh and blood factory producing, maintaining, and nurturing the **most important product of all, *people*.**

The *experts* agree saying, 'Yes, that's true. Many important economic sectors are omitted from the GDP. It's true, GDP is vastly understated.' Other *externalities* are: the *Underground* economy; the *Grey* market, *Asset-property* value; *Non-monetary* cashless barter-trading.

Also omitted from GDP are *subsistence production* and economic sectors such as the $3 trillion in *health care.*
The omission of *health care* amounts to denying the existence of a major portion of the 2014 GDP.

Estimates of annual unpaid housework average $70,000 per family. There are about 100 million families in the US. This would add another $7 trillion to the GDP if housework received wages. In 2014 GDP is estimated to exceed $17 trillion. Adding *externalities* such as *health care* and *housework* would nearly double GDP. One might consider the GDP a bumpy road going nowhere, as it attempts to ignore too many deep holes.

Households produce: *wageworkers*, *houseworkers*, *consumers*, *social class*, *human culture*, and even *people*. Some *experts* ask, 'Is the production of people a *social* or a *biological* act.' Most would say it's both.

The implication is that plants and animals are products of nature and do not qualify for inclusion in the GDP. This point would have some merit if it were not for tree, vegetable, grain, and fruit farming. Livestock farmers and animal breeders also qualify as both social and biological producers—all are products of nature, including people.

From a purely economic viewpoint, producing people amounts to producing the *means of production;* that is to say, producing the tools needed to produce everything else.

Social production: Raising children is a biological and social process. Childbirth is a natural process; but does not detract from its economic, social, and cultural value.

Factories reduce or increase production depending on demand. People may choose to produce fewer children during hard times, such as the *Great Depression/Recession.* People have more kids during prosperous times, as during the prosperous baby-boom period of 1945 to 1975. **Ignoring the economic significance of housework is an abusive assault on the family**. It denies workers their pay. It is criminal negligence.

As with racial and religious injustice, restitution is necessary to correct the situation. The injustice done to houseworkers is comparable to slave labor. Most would admit that the market economy cannot exist without wageworkers or houseworkers. Treasurers must ask themselves, 'Can humanity survive and progress without people, households, and families?'

12-Caere Astarte with lions 700 BC

By maintaining her step-family's social life-style, Cinderella produced middle class society, just as social ritual produces tribal society. If a subsistence-gathering form of production reproduces tribal society, then wagework-housework produces market society. The profit-

33

system being what it is, houseworkers produce their family, but also produce their own *underdevelopment*.

A further implication arises in that *production* and *reproduction* of people always occur within a *social* context. It's safe to say that all human activity is action within a *social context*. No person is an island.

The character of the family reflects the social influences that continually impact it. It's as if the family is a sheet of film. Constant exposure to the profit-economy imprints, socializes, and shapes every aspect of family.

People are embedded in social-economic environments and act in accord with it or suffer the consequences. Similarly, we must nurture our children to do the same.

Indoctrinating nuclear families: In the 1950's parents instructed children how to survive in a man's world:
1) People *must* work; they *must* have jobs or professions;
2) Men do interesting work for wages or salaries;
3) Women do uninteresting housework, earning no wages;
4) Women, not men, *must* marry and have children;
5) To survive, women *must* prepare for living in a man's world; women must be passive loving wives and mothers;
6) Women *must* adhere to these teachings more than men.
The 1950's *musts* fade as profit society self-destructs.

Household socialization: It was suggested, children are products of *spousal associations*, not the product of women or men. This fact is ignored by class society. Parents produce children and that is the most basic act of *social production* and housework. (Beatrice Ferneyhough, *On the Confinement of Women to Housework as an Exclusion from Social Production*, POLITICAL AFFAIRS)

Families as socially productive units within the profit-economy, depending on: 1) Women *socialized* to be subordinate to men; 2) Children's acceptance of market work relations; 3) Family as the center of consumption and production; consuming by converting wage income into household purchases; 4) Houseworkers are a hidden reserve work force of *unemployed-underemployed*, working in virtual isolation in the home; houseworkers are called out for wagework commodity production when labor shortages develop, as during major wars or economic crises.
http://en.wikipedia.org/wiki/Wages_for_housework

Within the profit-system houseworkers' household production is unique. *Socializing* people is no casual process. It's a **structured feedback system** between:
1) Parents, children, and media (TV, cable, and Internet);
2) Parents and government;
3) Work discipline, standards, values, and parents;
4) Children, peers, corporations and media (advertising);
5) Government and regulatory groups.

Housework-Wagework Production: For houseworkers to improve their productivity and working conditions they must leave the confinement of the household. This occurs when the family wageworker loses a job, forcing the houseworker to use household skills in wagework.

13-Astarte Olympia, Greece with lions 600 BC

Houseworkers typically find low-wage work in food, security, cleaning, sanitation, retail, office, and related jobs. As few employers hire full-time workers, most wageworkers are forced to accept a part-time job, often two or more part-time jobs are needed as most offer little more than eighteen hours of work per week. The trend is that three times more women and young people enter the job market compared to mature men.

Household skills are in demand by the low wage job market. Houseworkers cleaning their own home receive no wage; but cleaning more affluent households can earn up to $100 for three hours cleaning. As the word gets around, a resourceful house cleaner can clear $1000 per week. The double standard is obvious. Cleaning someone else's home is more rewarding than cleaning one's own.

Why is it *productive* to do the same work for others if it pays a wage and makes a profit? Why is doing our own housework considered *unproductive*?
The lack of housework status makes it difficult for a wageworker to do housework, unless housework is done by a woman.

14-Astarte of Capua, Italy with geese 500 BC

When a houseworker cares for the family wage earner, it is the employer who profits from both household and workplace labor. The employer only pays one wageworker, but gets housework labor at no extra cost.

Employers not only *skin the ox* twice, but three times: 1st, getting excess *productivity value* compared to the actual cost of production; 2nd, paying a *low wage,* often a thousand times less than the products produced; and 3rd, getting *free housework.*

The family consumes wage income; but employers consume both wagework and housework. Employers say, 'We pay for *performance* not for *ability*.' **If the real value of work were paid, there would be no profit.**

In the real world of drug production, there is the story of a worker paid $10 an hour to produce in one hour a drug that will sell for $500,000. This is typical drug industry economics.

Of course there are more costs involved than just wages. All costs factored in total $100. Net profits or return on investment, ROI, often reaches 5,000 to one in drug companies, ROI=5000:1. One industry exceeding drug ROIs are software companies selling over the Internet. A product costing a network buyer $100 can have an accounting cost of one cent or an ROI of 10,000 to one.

This is how the global pyramid of wealth is amassed: 99.8% at the base support 0.2 % at the top. Wage and house workers not only hold up 99.8% of the world, they hold up the super-wealthy 0.2% as well.

Years ago as a marketing manager, one of my product managers tried to market a veterinary drug that could only sell for ten times its cost.

We both knew what would happen; nevertheless we presented our plan to our vice president, my friend Bill. The product manager presented her plan and Bill smiled nodding supportively throughout the presentation. I asked Bill, 'So what's your verdict? What do you suggest?'

Bill replied smiling broadly, 'You knew the answer long before this presentation, which was excellent by the way. If the Swiss don't see at least a 1,000 fold ROI they'll tell us to sell the product to another company.'

A few years after the presentation, the drug company divested itself of everything but high ROI drugs. Eventually they went 100% into bio-genetic technology and realized truly obscene profits.

15-Sparta Astarte with lions 600 BC

Housework estrangement: The wretchedness of the worker is inversely proportional to the power and magnitude of worker's productivity. The more we produce outside the family, the less we have for our family, and the more wretched we become.

Considering wealth imbalance and cost-cutting, it's clear *Haves* benefit more from economic crises than prosperity. Husbands, and children through their loving involvement, and their loving blackmail, become the first foremen, the immediate controllers of labor.

This economic process involves the *estrangement* of houseworker and wageworker from family, as well as from society. Workers become separated from the results of their labor. This is the source of family *estrangement*.
During economic crises there is a substantial rise in divorce, separation, and family break-up.

People attempt to juggle housework and wagework, especially in times of economic crises. This occurs in much the same way as a boss manipulates work and workers.

In tribal, artisan, and cottage-craft society, production is limited but communal. Artisans control their own work. They knew what happened to their product; they consumed it; it did not leave their hands. As long as production remained this way, it could not become an alien power against them. (Frederick Engels, *The Origin of the Family, Private Property, and the State: in the light of the researches of Lewis H. Morgan;* Based on Morgan's *Ancient Society*)

Early family formation: The earliest human societies identified *male jealousy* as the vital problem to be controlled. For this reason *group marriage* emerged as the oldest form of family. Early tribal communes were based on matrilineal clans. Women lived with sisters, considering *my sister's child is my child.* Kinship solidarity empowered women to take action against uncooperative males.

40

The *world historic defeat of women* occurred with the slow shift from *mother-right* to *father-right*. It was the start of large-scale farming and herding 10,000 years ago; and resulted in increased male control of women in the home. http://en.wikipedia.org/wiki/Origin_of_the_Family

16-Hopi Corn Maid spirit 1,000 AD

6-HOUSEWORK PROFIT: *Now it happened that the king's son was giving two balls, to which all persons of fashion were invited. Of course the two young ladies received invitations, for they went out much into society.* (Charles Perrault *Cinderella* 1697)

The concept of *profit* is alien to early households; but concepts of *gain* are a natural part of family life. The distinction between *profit* and *gain* is significant.

Tribal people exchange *gifts* to strengthen social ties. Widespread *gift* exchange strengthens social bonds. *Gain* is part of tribal culture to the extent it is part of social exchange. Tribals *gain* status and prestige by gift giving. *Profit* as wealth from labor, is meaningless in tribal society.

41

Cinderella's Family: Viewing Cinderella as merely a household drudge misses an important point. A more significant picture emerges when considering the impact of market forces on the household.

Cinderella's servant status results as much from merchant culture as from the step-family. Cinderella and step-family social aspirations are creations of mercantile society. In the story, the father is absent most of the time, anticipating conditions that persist in 21st Century families.

In 1600's mercantile society, Cinderella and step-family realize their security and social ties depend on making the *right connections* at the ball. *Social ties* contribute to *gain* in all societies. A *good-marriage* is evaluated in terms of status *gain,* and *wealth.*

In the 21st Century, a *good-marriage* is defined similarly, but increasingly a *good-marriage* is a caring, loving, and long-term relationship. More often it's a *good-relationship*, rather than a *good-marriage* that provides high status.

Tribal and market trade: One South Pacific tribe, broadly spread among hundreds of miles and dozens of Solomon Island atolls, continues a complex pattern of social exchange. The exchange pattern involves passing gifts along in a network of islands: Island A, the Yam clan gives yams to island B, as part of a gift ritual lasting many days.

Island B and A clans are closely related. Island B has an abundance of coconuts to exchange with island C. Shark clan on Island C are skilled shark hunters and will exchange dried shark meat with the Tapa clan on Island D. The Tapa clan works a trade with the Boar clan.

These trades form a complex trading network. The complexity results from the fact that each clan may exchange dozens of items with considerable feedback. This example demonstrates:

1) Exchange is *social integration* for vast numbers of kin spread over a large area. Periodic trade provides a structured, orderly, and ritualized way of maintaining *social relations*. As part of the cycle, a bride or groom may be negotiated. The sick may be consigned to a medicine woman. A newborn child may be introduced.

2) A secondary value is filling the gaps in *clan needs* as no island or clan is fully self-sufficient. All clans need or desire something from other clans.

3) No market or quantitative exchange is involved. All trade is in the form of *gifts*. Clans know they will eventually have their needs met. These South Pacific clans practice *just exchange*, but *not quantitative* exchange. The idea that 100 pounds of yams is equivalent to ten yards of tapa is meaningless in this tribal exchange system.

Concepts of gain: The earliest link between concepts of *gain* is *gift exchange* to strengthen social ties. Gain as war booty and tribute has a minor role in tribal society.

Prior to the global profit-economy, wealth existed to increase household-clan-tribal *status*. Ancient society centered more on tribe-clan than family.

17-Astarte of Klazomenai, Greece with lions, 700 BC

In 500 BC Athens, the household family clan was virtually the entire economy. All economic-social functions were encompassed in tribal-clans. A clan consisted of a large number of kin, multiple generations, living on large tracts of land passed from earlier periods.

Aristotle referred to clan-households as **Oekonomi**, or self-sufficient households. *Economy* is the modern derivation. Tribal-clan-households resembled feudal kingdoms rather than families. Most **Oekonomi** were located in coastal areas, providing extensive sea-trade.

Oekonomi: In ancient society gifts were of two types. Most gift-exchange was between and within **Oekonomi.** Gifts

44

between **Oekonomi** were largely *social* and served to build or maintain *political* alliances as well as *trade*. The second type of gain was *tribute* from vassal **Oekonomi**. *Booty* from tribal war and *great adventure* was a marginal addition to **Oekonomi** gain.

Clan leaders would amass *social prestige* and fame by embarking on great adventures as in the *Odyssey, Iliad,* and *Aeneid*. Quests were feasible as clan leaders could leave the **Oekonomi** in charge of the clan matron, spouse, or close kin. Raiding adventures were typical of late Neolithic, Bronze Age, and post 1,500 BC patriarchs. The ten-year Greek-Trojan trade war occurred during this period.

From gift to profit: A profit economy can only be built by first destroying or absorbing a previous society. This process is more easily understood in terms of an actual family.

One clan of our tribe originates in an isolated part of the Austrian Alps. European upheavals during the mid-1800s prompted migration to Florida. Even with 200 years of assimilation much of our original culture is maintained.

Of particular interest is the complex pattern of *gifting*. A strong matriarchal culture persists. All major decisions are still made by mothers. Elder mothers have the most status. In clan gatherings elder matriarchs speaks first. Younger mothers speak in descending order of age. Men participate in discussions only when asked. Except for children, no one is permitted to leave the clan discussions.

Gifts are exchanged based on clan status. The oldest mother of each visiting household presents a gift to the host mother via the youngest child in the visiting family.

It's the person of least status that presents the gift to the highest status host mother. The implied *gift-message* is: 'this gift is unworthy of your status; but the youngest will present it as a token of our esteem.'

With the most recent generations of our clan, the *profit* motive has largely eclipsed the older *status* arrangements. Now it is *wealth* that holds the most status. Professional, educational, and business status replace what was in my youth an unquestioned matriarchal structure.

Patriarch restructuring converts a *social*-oriented kinship group into one that is now *money*-oriented. The clan is now fragmented into small nuclear families. Clan families are now focused on income rather than social relations.

Profit and labor: When the marketplace needs labor the final source is the household. If on the other hand there is an over-supply of workers, they are shifted back to the household.

This is the *reserve army* of houseworkers. It's especially true for women comprising over half the labor force.

Women are paid a lower wage than men. For this reason women are in demand in the labor force.

Women are attracted to wagework at two stages of the economic cycle: In *prosperous war* times, when men are unavailable and labor is in short supply; and during *boom* times.

During *down-turns*, when prices are high and wages cut, women replace higher paid men. During *down-turns,* cost-cutting reduces work hours and replaces full-time workers with part-time workers without benefits. Thus, most families need multiple part-time jobs to survive.

Housework super-profits: While the number of women wageworkers has greatly increased, wages have declined. This is true for all workers; but especially for women.

College educated women's income often lags behind male high school drop-outs. Increasingly, women are heads of households. In the 21st Century, half of U.S. families are headed by women. The drive to add millions of housewives to the labor force results in lower wages for women and men. As wages decline so do income and purchasing. This is why income cuts result in a *downward demand spiral*.

This is the reason global economies are trapped in a cost-cutting black-hole. The sequence is: pursuit of profits

47

motivates cost-cutting, lower-wages, leading to reduced income, reduced buying, and a down-ward economic spiral.

18-Astarte of Crete with geese 1,000 BC

The profit pyramid: Here's an example from my own corporate experience. My annual sales were $3 million; with a net corporate profit of $2.9 million after all expenses. The full cost of supporting my sales work was $60,000. This includes $30,000 in salary and $30,000 in corporate expenses, bonuses, fringe benefits, and overhead. Total sales rep cost is $60,000/$2,900,000 million or 2% of net corporate profit.

My pay was $15 an hour. Annual sales averaged $3,000,000 for 2,000 work hours or an annual return of $1,500 per hour, at a cost of $15 per hour pay. I received 1% of my sales. My 1% supports the 99% of cash produced for my employer. It amounts to a wealth pyramid for the 0.2% of super-rich, produced by 99.8% of workers.

Profit-economy uses household consumption to extract super-profits. In *Leaver* society, *needs had finite limits*.

48

19-Astarte of Vetulonia, Greece with vixen 500 BC

Nuclear family needs are exactly opposite. The profit-economy promotes unlimited needs. Encouraging a flood of buying is an attempt to substitute *things* for *social* relations.

Craving *stuff* is thought to fill the gaps in *social* relations. People are coerced into filling their social void with *things*. Why do millions spend weekends at the mall? At least window shopping is affordable even if buying is not.

We pretend to be part of a great tribe of brand-name shoppers. Only a valid credit card is needed. Media and social pressure drive the engine of consumption. *Shopping* provides *social contact* to ease our loneliness.

20-Ephesus Astarte with lions, pottery shard 1,000 BC

The most frightening aspect of the profit-economy is its relation to the environment. Tribal societies adapt to their environment. As with the Mbuti, most tribal people are at

49

peace with nature, taking what they need and leaving the rest. They are the *Leavers*.

Profit-economy is at war with nature. Profit culture has an insatiable appetite for consuming the world. They are the *Takers*.

7-PRODUCTIVE CONSUMPTION: *Cinderella was kept busy washing, ironing, and sewing for them.* (Charles Perrault, *Cinderella)*

Perhaps the most contradictory aspect of market society is consumption. In 21st Century society we are saturated with media pressure to shop, buy, and consume.

Luxuries and necessities: Media exists to sell *stuff*. When *Have-nots* are assaulted with TV ads for *stuff* they want, but can't afford, it's like pressure building in a boiler. The problem is that trivial luxuries are readily available while necessities are not. People with low income, especially the young, are driven by media to crave *stuff*, but are denied the means to satisfy cravings.

Faced with the step-family's craving for luxury, while Cinderella wears rags, the story reaches the boiling point with an invitation to the ball.

Cinderella's deprivation is the price she pays for step-family indulgence in luxury. Unpaid labor of *Have-nots*, such as houseworkers like Cinderella, supports the conspicuous consumption of step-family *Haves*.

Is consumer freedom a cruel myth? To choose between different packages of soap is more a reflection of corporate power than consumer freedom. Decisions about what to produce, distribute, and sell rests with corporations, rather than consumers.

Freedom to sell packages of *less* for *more* does not increase consumer freedom. It demonstrates the power to deceive, while insisting consumers are free to choose. As profits rise, consumer freedom shrinks along with income and what families can afford to buy.

Cinderella lives a life of drudgery, consuming the bare minimum. Is she content with the crumbs of life?

21-Rhodes Astarte with lion and deer, 300 BC

Cinderella is the ideal profit-system worker; she does the most housework for the least pay. She might be called the *zero-point* worker as she gets the least to do the most.

Private indulgence and public need: Mounting conflict between the *public* needs of the 99.8% and *private* wealth

of the 0.2% is reaching the crisis point. To satisfy private needs for autos, homes, smartphones, and other stuff, public funds and taxes are appropriated for roads, gas, electricity, water, sanitation, and wireless cell towers.
This is yet another way the 0.2% extracts income from the 99.8%. It's all for the public good, of course.

When corporations cut wage income, they view their employees as the *help*, but see everyone else as *customers*. Expanding profit depends on expanding production and consumption on three levels. *Increasing profit requires*:
1) Increasing population, households, and *consumption*;
2) Increasing *existing demand* via media marketing;
3) Increasing demand via *fashion, innovation, education, health care*, and *environmental* fixes.

22-Syracuse Astarte with goat 400 BC

As *Takers* invest in space-travel, profits become cosmic in scope. Consumption still depends on *Leavers* working and shopping here on Earth.

Now with over half the work force made up of women, the housework spouse is as likely to be a woman as a man.

Housework is now performed by the person spending the most time at home. The houseworker remains the primary shopper. Without houseworkers, expanding consumption is at risk.

Shrinking consumption is the result of shrinking income. Less income means less buying. The 99.8% with shrinking income are *Leavers*. As income shrinks, debt, and resentment expand.

Consumption: Consumer demand directs production, just as production directs consumption. The vital part of consumption is buying more *stuff*. It seems simple, but it's not. The complexity of profit makes everything complex.

23-Amlash Fertility Goddess, open-arm button face, Iran 1,000 BC

Housework produces people before they become producers. Cinderella *consumes* to produce herself, prior to *producing* a step-family. She discovered *productive-consumption*.

8-WEALTH OF NATIONS: *The prince was constantly at her side, paying her compliments and speaking tender words to her. But it*

was twelve o'clock! Cinderella jumped up and ran, swiftly as a deer.
(Charles Perrault, *Cinderella*)

Housework and Capital: Wikipedia defines *Capitalism* as an economic system of trade, industry, labor, and tools of production *privately* owned and operated for *profit*. *Capital* is property *ownership*. The key words are: *privately owned property*, and *profit*. http://en.wikipedia.org/wiki/Capitalism

Profit is *gain* as income exceeds: expenses, costs, and taxes needed to sustain a business. Profit gained belongs to owners. Profit may be distributed publicly or kept privately. Profit distribution is the key issue, not profit itself. http://en.wikipedia.org/wiki/Profit

All assets including people begin in the family and are the result of housework. The origin of capital, property, ownership, profit, and wagework is family housework.

Housework and capital stand at opposite ends of the production process. At one end is capital, bringing workers and tools together; extracting surplus labor from workers over and above wages; and converting part of the surplus labor into profit. At the other end is housework producing and nurturing all workers. Capital *extracts* labor, tools, and skills from people produced by family housework.

Capital is the power of corporate-banking over of our lives. Capital converts family farms into factory farms; and transforms household crafts into industrial production.

54

Natural family: Primates, felines, and hominids appeared at the end of the Miocene period 5-million years ago. *Natural* family refers to the earliest human social formations 3 to 5 million years ago.

What we now consider *family* was preceded by human *hordes*, *bands*, *clans*, and *tribes*. These were migrating hunter-gathers.

24-Corneto Astarte 500 BC

The success of early humans depended on small slow-growing population.

Little more than 250 people can be supported in hunter-gather groups. Hunter-gatherers *spin-off* groups to neighboring areas once the population exceeds 250 people.

Australopithecus such as *Lucy* is about 5-million years old. *Lucy* was probably one of hundreds of evolving *Lucys* appearing in primate bands over a period of 1,000 years.

These new primates eventually formed their own bands and hordes on the emerging African savannahs. At first, *Lucys* may have followed the baboon social pattern, creating their own *mother-centered* social groups.

As with primates and many animals, the first humans likely evolved from primates in Africa. Neanderthal, early

Homo sapiens, may be 1-million years old, preceding *Modern* humans into the Middle East half a million years ago. Modern people evolved in Africa 100-200 thousand years ago, migrating to the Middle East 50,000 years ago.

As long as human population remained small and the environment permitted, natural groups lived a relatively abundant hunter-gather life style for 3-million years.

In the first 190,000 years, *Modern* humans are thought to have doubled their numbers every 19,000 years, from 10,000 to 10-million. Over the last 10,000 years, improved farming and livestock skills resulted in the so-called *agricultural revolution.* Eating of the knowledge tree, we left our garbage in the garden. *Leavers* became *Takers.*

25-Capua Astarte with lions, 400 BC

Autarky lives! Family and human transformation is a long, slow, and painful process. To understand the transformation we need to distinguish between pre-capitalist tribal society and profit-society. *Autarky* refers to self-sufficient and independent tribal society prior to global

56

mercantile society. The *Cinderella* story reflects the transition from pre-capitalist to capitalist family.

Autarkic families were clans, tribes, medieval farming communes, and cottage-craft communities. Some continue to prosper in the 21st Century. In particular, Hutterite, Amish, and Mennonite groups populate North America.

Creating nuclear families: Early entrepreneurs were few and like most minorities carefully avoided confrontations with those in power. As inward-looking feudal society self-destructed, merchants looked outward to a new world of global trade, innovation, and exchange of ideas. In spite of plagues that killed off a large portion of Europeans, global mercantile trade and immigration rapidly built a new invigorated Europe.

As church and royals destroyed themselves with endless wars, new merchant-princes filled the space in a severely depopulated Europe. Global mercantile trade transformed successful merchants into even more successful capitalists.

With the exception of religious societies such as Hutterites, capital changed the world into a profit-society. Marxists say capitalism is a vast improvement over feudalism and slavery, providing a new culture of enterprise, liberty, and freedom; while at the same time institutionalizing greed, corruption, and mendacity. Even limited freedom has its price. To survive, *Leavers* became *Takers*. Tribal clans transformed into nuclear families.

In spite of the undeniable liberating effects of capitalism, the profit-economy has an infinite capacity to separate people from each other.

26-**Astarte of Milesia**, Greece with lions 600 BC

On the one hand, capital liberated people; but the profit-system also destroyed family and social cohesion.

9-BIRTH of PROPERTY:

Prior to patriarchal society a culture of personal *land-ownership* did not exist. While tribal *communal land* occupation and personal property were accepted since antiquity, *personal land ownership* was not.

The economic power of markets and property became viable over the last 10,000 years, via farming and population increase. Patriarchal tribes dominated south Europe 2,500 years ago.

The process of domination was gradual over 1,500 years. It resulted in matriarch-tribal *communal* land slowly

58

replaced by patriarch *personal* land ownership. In tribal society one could no more buy or sell land than sell their mother. Tribal land was communal, not a commodity.

By the time the Latin tribes of the early Roman Republic became the Tribal Assembly; the Latin tribes were little more than congressional voting districts as in the U.S. The democratic Roman Tribal Assembly of the early republic was gradually weakened. It was powerless by the time Caesar Augustus became the first Emperor in the new era.

Before the idea of *land-property* could gain credence it was necessary to weaken the tribal power of Greek *Oikonomia* and Roman *Familia*. Both *Oikonomia* and *Familia* included all kin, retainers, supporters, friends, soldiers, and slaves. The great Italian families such as the Borgia, Medici, and Sforza were created on the model of the old Roman *Familia*.

27-Alexandria Astarte with geese 800 BC

Slavery begins with war captives. Slaves taken in battle were usually integrated into Greek *Oikonomia* or Roman *Familia*. Slaves were often part of the family retinue. In most of the ancient world slaves were usually war booty, foreigners, debtors, and criminals.

With the advent of patriarchs, houseworkers are treated as slaves, to the extent it is unpaid coerced labor. The low status of housework rises as self-employed houseworkers are paid to do housework.

Women see themselves as household slaves to the extent they are confined to housework, rather than life outside.

As with Cinderella, we prefer stories about household liberation, rather than household servitude. Advertising features the themes of '*freedom* from household drudgery; give mom a break; the all-purpose detergent that *frees* you from wash-day misery.' It's all media hype. The profit-system *liberates* houseworkers only for wagework.

Society without property: In hunter-gather societies sustenance depends on natural resources. Foraging works in equatorial rain forests. In regions such as the Amazon and Ituri forests, women and children often gather twice as much food as hunters.

In contrast to *gathering* societies, *accumulating* cultures work best where Mother Nature is less generous. Temperate, grassland, savannah, desert, arctic, and hill-mountain terrain are typical of *accumulating* societies.

The concept of *land-property* begins where farming and herding take hold. Land competition arises between farmers and herders. Cain and Abel set the stage for a contentious future between farmer and herder, urban and rural, expansionists and tribals—between *Takers* and *Leavers*.

Conflict between farmers and cattlemen persist. Clashes over *landed property* began with the large-scale farming. Global conflict continues as transnational corporations expand to conquer nature and markets.

Farmers and herders covet each other's land. The story of Cain and Abel represents the clash between farmers and herders. As was the case in the 19th Century American west, farmers and cattlemen fought over land, water, and other resources. Barb-wire was the *Taker* solution.

Hollywood westerns are based on the struggle to control land, water, and competitors such as bison and Native Americans. What was once *communal tribal land* and open-range was fenced-off *private property,* reservations, and nature preserves.

In harsh areas, people attempt to adjust or move on. That was the case with *Modern Homo sapiens* forced out of East Africa 50,000 years ago. Over thousands of years, the change to a hot dry climate forced migration into the Middle East. New generations leap-frogged over the old.

Hunter-gathers could not stay long in areas of dwindling resources. For our ancestors, their *only home was change.* The idea of *property* formed slowly; requiring the experience of savagery and barbarism to germinate, and to prepare the human brain for endless expansion.

Humans followed the grazers, following the vegetation along shrinking water-ways. The great cats followed the followers. As seen in the graphics of Astarte with lions, cats and people follow the survival trail together.

In sparse regions, early herders found it necessary to accumulate whatever food was available. Early on they dried, smoked, salted, spiced, and stored many foods.

Environmental stress creates the notion of property, especially herding. Stages of human development correspond to divisions of labor: gathering, hunting, herding, farming, and combinations of these. Divisions of labor correspond to forms of ownership and property.

Narrow expansionist greed now dominates all other passions. It marks the end of profit culture and hopefully the rebirth of humane civilization. (Emmanuel Terray's summary of T. E. Morgan's *Primitive Societies*)

Household property: Few people enjoyed a naturally *affluent* environment. The first divisions between housework and other work become *specialized* as a result of climate and environmental stress.

Work and technology evolved with the need for specialized food preparation and storage. Child-care and education fell into one category of *specialized* work. Herding, hunting, and raiding were other areas of specialty.

While Viking raiders were farmers during the short Scandinavian growing season, they pillaged Europe the rest of the year. One of the earliest real estate scams was selling parcels of what Vikings called Greenland, a land that's never green. They kept *green* Iceland for themselves.

Typically, property rights followed tribe and clan ownership. Women of one clan had their own skills, tools, and property, as did men of a different clan. Division of labor followed along the lines of clan, skill, and need.

28-Crete Earth Mother with lions 1,800 BC

When *property* was created, slavery arrived violating all tribal principles of equal rights, personal freedom, and democracy. Slavery was sustained by greed and the delusion that the person made a slave was a blood stranger and captive enemy. With *property* also came the notion of aristocracy, privileged status, and class superiority.
(Emmanuel Terray's summary of T. E. Morgan's *Primitive Societies*)

Ceremonial property: Many tribes observe: taboos, totems, fetishes, talismans, ritual artifacts, and other forms of ceremony. These are observed in tribes such as Canadian Pacific coast Kwakiutl, who are probably the most affluent of all tribes. Their lands are secured for them by the Canadian government. Kwakiutl society is based primarily on fishing; while men hunt, and women gather.

Ornate weaving and woodwork were important crafts, and wealth, defined by slaves and material goods, was prominently displayed and traded at potlatch ceremonies.

Wealth and status were not determined by how much you had, but by *how much you gave away*. Northwest Pacific Coast tribes had a well-developed property concept; but did not expand into other tribal areas. Hunting and fishing land was inherited. Property wealth was collected distributed, and destroyed in potlatch rituals.

In the 21st Century, Northwest Pacific tribes continue to enjoy dense forests and sea coasts teaming with salmon, fur, redwoods, and other wealth. All of this bounty is primarily for building tribal status and prestige.

29-Alert Bay Totems 1900;
30-Potlatch totems and ritual masks;
31-Kwagu'ł noble-woman with royal abalone shell earrings;
32-A Copper in the characteristic 'T' http://en.wikipedia.org/wiki/Kwakiutl

Ritual Wealth: Totems, painted *big-houses,* ritual masks, coppers, jewelry, dances, and woven textiles become integral parts of ritual wealth, providing clan status. Burning *potlatch* wealth is now forbidden.

Depending on marriage and clan status, individuals may *own* special designs, songs, and dances. To gain high status an *important* person must hold a *potlatch*. Wool blankets serve as traditional exchange wealth. Totem artists are paid thousands of dollars for clan totems that may rise higher than a three-story building.

Tribal wealth: Haida of the Alaska Coast are perhaps the foremost among tribal cultures. Along with a preeminent artistic culture, Haida are traditionally the most aggressive and acquisitive of tribal groups.

Tribal society takes pride in the unity of people, household, family, clan, and tribe. Tribal unity is the goal of complex ritual and ceremony. Acceptance of the natural environment is part of tribal culture.

Profit-society is the opposite of tribal, conquering nature to expand profits. In the process, family and society are divided into smaller units to expand consumption and profits. Profit society gains from inequalities and divisions.

In contrast, tribal society is extended family seeking unity; while profit-society seeks family division.

Class distinctions: Creating inequality and division in profit-society results in class distinctions. Criteria contributing to class distinctions include:
Wealth *Favors* Rich; *Discriminating* against Poor;
Sex *Favors* Men; *Discriminating* against Women;
Race *Favors* White; *Discriminating* against Color;
Age *Favors* Prime; *Discriminating* against Old.
Class divisions are based on: housework/wagework, wives/husbands, urban/rural, and Takers/Leavers.

66

As family wealth increases, class distinctions also increase. In profit society, *patriarch status* imposes itself at the top of a wealth pyramid, supported by the rest of us. This is why the distinction between the super-rich 0.2% of *Haves* and the other 99.8% of *Have-nots* is compared to a pyramid of wealth. The growing concentration of wealth depends on dividing households, houseworkers, and wageworkers. The isolation is economic, social, and physical.

This may explain why families continue to shrink in size while becoming more numerous. More households mean more consumption and tighter control by the *Haves*.

Plutonomies: describe the current global trend of rule by *super-rich* plutocrats.

39-Geometric Mother Goddess, Predmost Moravia 40,000 BC

There is a strong long-term trend toward more concentrated wealth. This trend largely results from *plutonomy-friendly governments* and *taxes*; suggesting *plutonomies* buy governments via lobbyists and political contributions.

Plutocrats have a net worth of at least $30 million. In 2013 there were 199,235 plutocrats globally, worth $27.77 trillion. There were 2,170 billionaires in the world, with a combined net worth of $6.5 trillion. Billionaires represent 23% of total global wealth.

If there are 2-billion global families, with a little over three people per family, then the 0.2 million global *Have* families are but one out of 10,000 families. Imagine a pyramid of wealth consisting of 9,999 families supporting one family. This is the image of the massive social instability we face.

Equality versus inequality: East Asian nations with fairly *even income distribution* dramatically outperformed Latin American countries with *less equal income distribution.*

Investment in nutrition, health, and education of poor children produced more economic opportunity and higher economic performance. Research studies suggest *inequality may have adverse effects,* blunting productive incentives and fueling costly conflicts between *Haves* and *Have-nots.*
http://en.wikipedia.org/wiki/Samuel_Bowles_(economist)

In 2013, *super-rich* global wealth, of 15,000 households, increased by 20%; controlling 5.5% of global wealth (one-third live in the US). The trend toward wealth concentration is likely to continue unabated. *Sub-millionaire* wealth is likely to increase by 3.7% annually until 2019.

The *super-rich* growth rate is 9.1%. *Super-rich* are expected to gain a 6.5% share of global wealth by 2019.

There is a risk that since political enfranchisement remains as one person, one vote, it's likely labor will fight back, resulting in a political backlash against the rising power of wealth. http://en.wikipedia.org/wiki/Ultra_high-net-worth_individual

Cinderella's story reflects the conflict between small urban nuclear family and the large rural family. The antagonism between *Have* and *Have-not* families continues to grow into a major conflict.

10-HAVES and HAVE-NOTS: *Cinderella was called upon to help and advise them, for she had excellent taste. She arranged their hair expertly even though they cruelly teased her.* (C. Perrault, *Cinderella*)

It's hard to imagine concepts of property and ownership where food and other resources are abundant. *Abundance* makes stock-piling pointless. Herding culture is more likely in regions of *scarcity*. Hunting and herding require more mental effort than gathering.

In an environment of *scarcity*, hardship shapes society and culture. Patriarchy, property, and inequality may be the result of *scarcity*. The scarcity of nature is often made more severe by man-made *scarcity*.

In *The Greek Myths*, Robert Graves gathered tales of Indo-European migrations to Europe starting 4,000 years ago.

40-Athens Artemis with chiton shawl and flower scrolls 525 BC

Major family changes occurred when *affluent* gathering societies were transformed into *scarcity* societies. Gatherer-hunter tribal societies depend on *equal* contribution from all and to all. The patriarchal family is one of dependence rather than independence.

In profit-society, labor is transformed into fragmented specialized housework and wagework. Not that the profit-system invented this situation, but it greatly expanded, rigidified, and institutionalized these conflicts, internalizing these in the germ of the nuclear family.

42-Paleolithic Bush People Fertility figures 20,000 BC

Status in profit-society is based on property and wealth. A wageworker providing the sole household income must support herself and those who do not bring home income.
Social status: In tribal society power relations focus on *people*. Most tribal societies attempt to strengthen social ties rather than accumulate *wealth*. While tribes may trade outside for mates, food, and other resources, the purpose is usually to build *status,* rather than *wealth*.

One of the more bizarre trades involves the Mbuti, the pygmy people of the Congo Ituri forest. Each year they spend a few months as *mock-slaves* of a market-oriented tribe living at the edge of the Ituri forest. This false servitude provides the Mbuti with metal weapons and tools.

The ferocious Win Tchan tribe of Chamgei, Thailand grows opium for sale to outsiders. Members of this slash and burn jungle tribe often take jobs in Bangkok and send money back to the tribe. Their dealings with the outside world are to obtain sophisticated weapons to preserve their isolated tribal society.

71

Exchange value: The earliest value system arose in primal band and tribal society. *Anarchic Subsistence* was the earliest *primal horde* social system. These were independent bands of primate kin, such as baboons. They were mother-child centered, surrounded by other females. Males protected the periphery. (Evelyn Reed, *Woman's Evolution*)

Same species primates of different hordes were considered *animals* and threats to be cannibalized. Early social systems including *outsiders* were mating and trade *alliances* with neighboring *Homo-habilis*, *Erectus*, and *Neanderthal*, beginning three million years ago.

Taboo-totem, as part of the *first value system*, was probably the last phase of the *primal horde*. This period included *Australopithecus* 5-million years ago.

The *primal horde* was a maternal grouping of mothers, sisters, children, and brothers, preceding the maternal clan. The horde stood alone without links to other groups of the same species. In contrast, more advanced tribal clans, or extended families, affiliate to form larger tribes.

The first primate rule was to *hunt-out* for food or mates. Mating-marriage *within* horde or clan was discouraged. Both horde and clan were *exogamous*. Intermarriage *outside* the clan arrived with the first connubial agreement between *exogamous* clans.

Incest households: In spite of *exogamy*, incest is an accepted and even preferred type of mating by some of the least developed as well as the most sophisticated tribes.

Exogamy was the rule in matriarchal society. In the transition to patriarchy, brother-sister marriage was preferred in Egypt, Iran, among the Java Kalanga, and with the Murung of Borneo. The Kalanga believe mother-son mating results in the most desirable offspring. Female groups would lose their unity if daughters moved out and alien women brought in. (Helen Diner, *Mothers and Amazons)*

42-Egyptian Hippopotamus Goddess 3,000 BC

Exogamy in early society proved essential for the preservation of matriarchal clans. In addition, *exogamy* strengthened the gene-pool. Usually older women enforced *exogamy*. Biological families protected and preserved maternal rights. Transition from matriarchy to patriarchy enforced *property* rights, inheritance, and male power.

In Egypt up to 200 AD, all inheritance was from mother to daughter. It was advantageous for Egyptian brothers and sisters to marry in order to keep property within the family.

73

Patriarchal stimulus for Egyptian brother-sister marriage affected all classes for thousands of years.

Totem and taboo: Mothers were the first law-givers. Survival laws preserved mother and child. Early taboos separated hunters from women and children to limit *blood lust* persisting after the hunt. Separation of women and children from men during meals was common for the same reason. Isolation of pregnant and menstruating women was also a frequent practice to reduce the sight and scent of blood that might excite *blood lust* in men.

Our intense repulsion for cannibalism is an inherited food taboo. In addition, many animals and plants are still rejected as food. Beans were rejected as spirit incarnations. Hardly a society can be found without some food taboo.

The cow is a well-known food taboo among ancient Egyptians, Phoenicians, and Hindus. Jews and Muslims abhor pork. Congo Banziris eat dogs. Zorastrians will not eat dogs. Dyak reject eels, but eat snakes. Bantus eat no fish. The taboo list is quite long.

Remnants of our cannibal past persist in blood-brotherhood rites. The Christian wafer-wine remains a token of Christ's flesh and blood. All such rites are celebrations of progress from savagery to civilization.

Gift exchange: Tribal society developed ritual value systems of gift exchange to maintain and strengthen social unity. Gift exchange is a global value system and is the core of most tribal culture. Gift exchange is part of marriage, ritual, celebration, and ceremony.

Tribal exchange is seldom thru markets; rather it is thru clan or tribal intermediaries. *Exchange* is not so much *things* as it is *social*: in the form of mates, courtesies, children, assistance, rituals, dance, songs, festivities, and feasts. Violating exchange rites often causes conflicts. *Gifting* is the central activity in most tribal societies.

43-Hopi pottery ancient Corn Mother 1,000 AD

Visiting, hunting, gathering, and cultivation are accompanied with an exchange of gossip, stories, and other social exchange. **Gift exchange is now family sharing and cooperation.**

Among Northwest Pacific coast tribes there is feast upon feast. When a marriage occurs, on ritual occasions, and on social advancement, there may be reckless consumption of

75

everything that was amassed with great effort from some of the richest coasts in the world. Clans are invited when a seal is killed. Everyone is invited when a whale runs aground. (Evelyn Reed, *Women's Evolution*)

Cases of blankets, fish, and even houses are burnt. The most valuable coppers are broken and thrown into the sea; until virtually all wealth is consumed, burnt, and transferred, leaving status seekers with nothing but status. Gift exchange is a form of insurance against *blood revenge*, demanding a life for a life. Gift exchange depends on placing a high value on life. It is a way of continually relieving hostility and loss of life.

Gift and head count: Iroquois hold tobacco as sacred; a gift bestowed on them by the creator. Fire is a sacred offering, a pledge of heart, mind, and sincerity. Iroquois regard the *vital harvest* as gifts of the creator held in great esteem. The *vital harvest* consists of food staples such as the *Three-Sisters*: corn-beans-squash, as well as the juice of forest berries and maple sap. Such foods are ritually imbued with a spirit of reverence.

Totems and taboos arose naturally as the first *laws*, protecting people and their food supply. Totem kin were under taboo not to kill or eat other totem kin. At first this restraint applied only to *primal horde* men.

76

Tribes observed: *animals as a rule, and all plants, do not feed on their own kind.* Grub men refused to eat grubs; grass men ate no grass seed, and so on through all the other totems. The struggle against cannibalism begins with totem-taboo. Most tribes and clans provide sanctuary for some animal or plant. (Evelyn Reed, *Woman's Evolution*)

Tribal gift exchange is the basis of human values. *Gifting* is the basis of *increase* rituals such as *Thanksgiving.* Increase rites included *fertility*—gifts of children, livestock,

44-Hopi Snake Goddess petroglyph 1,000 AD

and harvest. Gift, totem, and taboo build tribal-clan unity, especially for mate exchange.

S*eepage* in tribal groups results in killings. Iroquois *gifting* and *indenture* provide redress. To diffuse hostility a tally system was needed. Heads were an early accounting system to track loss of life.

A *headman* kept these grisly scores. Accurate count is little valued; but in the case of lives owed by one tribe to another, head counts were scrupulously maintained.

77

Shrinking and drying heads became a way of ritual counting tribal losses. Some South Pacific tribes displayed baskets of heads. The practice of *head-hunting* can be viewed as humane when understood in terms of limiting kills. Eventually, heads are refined into symbolic jewelry. The first accountants were headmen keeping headcounts.

A north India Walong native wore a necklace of three wooden heads, in memory of his three murdered brothers. The pendant reminded him that he had still to avenge his brothers' deaths. (Evelyn Reed, *Women's Evolution*)

When a murder is avenged, the murderer is eaten as part of a great celebration feast and the wood head is burnt. Tribal ornaments may be viewed as symbols of peaceful transition from *savage* to *social* life. Such necklaces replace *blood revenge*, as a major step-up from savagery.

The *headcount* was an important achievement as it limits reprisals. Jibaro of the Amazon will not kill more than one enemy, even when the opportunity exists to kill many. Eventually baskets of food replaced baskets of heads. *Life exchange* gradually replaced *death exchange*.

Later one person was sacrificed in place of all other deaths, as in the Crucifixion. Rather than symbols of wealth and property, tribal ornaments have great spiritual value confirming the monumental achievement of *gift-exchange over death-exchange.*

When two Andaman Island friends meet, the first thing they do is exchange gifts. In every-day village life there is constant gift giving and receiving. It's a breach of good manners to refuse one's request. In this way, Andaman possessions are constantly changing hands.

Transition from tribal *gifting* to feudal *bartering* is typical of 1,000-1,300 AD early mercantile trade. On a reduced level, *gifting* and *bartering* persist into the 21st Century.
(Evelyn Reed, *Women's Evolution*)

Origin of price: Tribal concepts of price and property exist only insofar as *social-status* gift exchange is concerned. Now *Social-exchange* is replaced by *hoarding wealth.*

45-Hopi Maiden-Goddess hair whorls, pottery cameo 1,000 AD

Scarcity, war, nation-states, and taxes undermine tribal society, as well as family structure. *Social-exchange* is eclipsed by profit, money, wage, and price. When laborers do wagework they exchange their abilities for another commodity, money. By transforming work into commodities, human labor is bought and sold like sacks of potatoes. Price, money, and market involve a peculiar equation in which *quality of living* is transformed into a *quantity of labor*.

Marketplace transforms people into labor fragments. The result is to place the social value of paid wageworkers above unpaid houseworkers.

Human commodities: Establishing a *price* sets-off a chain of conflicts, since price involves power relations. To get a *price* of $4.00 a bushel for corn that is $3.75 reflects corn scarcity. Grain brokers have power over the increased demand for corn. They have power over the corn buyer-consumer—a frequent event in both India and America.

By manipulating *price*, large suppliers can force small competitors out of the market. *Price* is a powerful club used to subdue the weak. *Haves* use their power to manipulate price, supply, value, and demand, at the expense of *Have-nots*.

In this regard the *price* of wagework is easily determined by manipulating supply-demand-production. This places housework at the lowest rung on the economic ladder, as housework is unpaid labor.

In profit-society there is a tendency to make money the measure of all value, including work; but most houseworkers receive no wage.

Since urban wageworkers labor outside the household, urban houseworkers cannot feel a part of a money-making team. In farm families, houseworkers usually feel they are part of the team. Many houseworkers believe their work would not be appreciated unless it was rewarded with pay. (Robert W. Smuts, *Women, and Work in America*)

In profit-society, status and prestige is based on income. Low housework status is based on low or no wages. The paradox in profit-society is that the *most important work,* producing *people,* is the least valued.

46-Hopi Corn Maiden, Shalako Mana 1,000 AD

U.S. Bureau of Labor Statistics values annual housework at $70,000. (Paul Meinhardt, *Cinderella's Housework*)

47-Hopi Earth Woman Ha-hai-wug-ti the trickster 1,000 AD

11-Our only home is *change*: *Cinderella, who was watching and who knew her own slipper, said lightly, 'let me see if it will fit.'*

Households originate in *pre-human* kinship groups. Primate mother-child nurture is the first *household.*

The Pliocene, 5-million years ago, is the likely origin of early humans such as *Australopithecus.* Global cooling spurred forest decline and the spread of savannas, forcing early humans onto grassland and out of dying forests. (http://en.wikipedia.org/wiki/Pliocene_climate)

Heating-drying forests forced primates to seek refuge at the waters' edge, the littoral. Out of the protective forests, primates were no match for the great cat predators.

One theory suggests the great cats eliminated less savvy primates as they left the forests. More intelligent primates survived to breed by out-smarting predatory cats. In this way cats aided human evolution.

Early humans survived by observing cats hunting the grazers. Humans saw how the great cats waited in tactical hunting groups, selecting weak or injured stragglers.

The first people probably ate what the cats left from their hunt. Later hunters let cats catch grazers, and then routed the cats with fire. Later still, cats might feed on what the people left, as they do today. People and cats hunted separately until people and domesticated cats, such as cheetahs, hunted together.

The first *modern* humans, perhaps 200,000 years ago, got the brilliant idea of capturing new-born feline kits to domesticate. Cats may have aided the creation of *modern* humans, as people created modern cats.

There's another dimension to the co-evolution of cats and people. It is a microscopic coccidian parasite known as *toxoplasma*, or *toxo*. *Toxo* affects mice, cats, and human brains. The main source of human infection is raw meat such as lamb. Handling cat feces is a major risk, especially for pregnant women, as *Toxo* may injure the fetal nervous system. http://en.wikipedia.org/wiki/Toxoplasmosis

Up to a third of global people carry the *Toxo* infection. *Toxo* first infects mice. Mice are attracted to cat urine, infecting cats, and finally people. *Toxo* can only reproduce in cats.

Toxo may increase hormone secretion of oxytocin, serotonin, dopamine, and endorphin in the brains of people, cats, and mice. This results in a mutual attraction. Hormone attraction may explain how cats and people are mutually attracted to each other; and similarly mice to cats.

Toxo can cause neural ills such as: attention deficit hyperactivity disorder, schizophrenia, suicidal behavior, and also other mental health disorders.

Three million years ago, ancestral primates were forced by forest transition to grassland, and big cats, to seek refuge in water-ways. As long as pre-humans could wade up to their necks, a measure of safety was gained. Solar mutations were more likely at the *littoral*, where water and land meet. Solar radiation is greater in water than sheltering forests.

Many *semi-aquatic* generations later, specific adaptive changes and mutations occurred. Thousands of years of precarious *littoral* life transformed forest and savannah primates into aquatics, with improved intelligence.

Remodeled apes evolved from *Australopithecus*. Gorilla, chimpanzee, and bonobo primates provided the genes from which *aquatic* pre-humans evolved.

Pliocene adaptive stress includes: heat, drought, solar radiation, and predators all seeking the waters' edge. *Humanizing* mutations shaped the pre-human and human household.

48-Willendorf Venus Earth-Mother Fertility figure, limestone 28,000–25,000 BC, http://en.wikipedia.org/wiki/Willendorf_Venus

The mutations are unique to marine mammals. Of all primates, these mutations are found only in humans: http://en.wikipedia.org/wiki/Elaine_Morgan_(writer)

1) *Pendulous breasts* are found only in marine mammals such as humans, bovines, elephants, pigs, and hippos, providing mother-child floatation and balance in water;

2) *Long thick hair* provides a hand-hold for children floating near the mother's shoulders

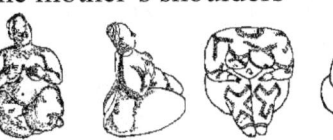

49-52 Large Breast Fertility votives of Çatalhöyük 6,000 BC

3) *Finger webs* serve as wading paddles; no other primate has 90 degree thumb-forefinger webbing;

4) Fat layer under the skin provides padding, insulation, and energy reserves for mother and child;

5) *Skin-hair patterns* ease water draining and mobility;

6) *Nasal-cartilage* seals-off lungs for diving under water;

7) *Facial frowning* shields eyes from reflected sunlight;

8) *Heart beat* slows under water;

9) *Salt tears* remove excess salt from the body;

10) *Flat feet* aid paddling and treading water;

11) *Steatopygia* buttock *shelf,* support infants;

53-Steatopygia grain bin fertility goddess, Çatalhöyük 6,500 BC

54-Steatopygia pregnant votive, Grottes de Grimaldi 30,000 BC
55-Steatopygia tattooed figure of Hacilar, Turkey, 6,000 BC

12) *Large body* size is unique to marine mammals;
13) *Vagina upright forward withdrawn* reduces injury;
14) *Larger penis* in humans compared to other primates;
15) *Front-mounting coitus* found only in marine mammals;
16) *Speech* is the only practical water communication;
18) *Infants Swim at birth* and are attracted to water.
These mutations suggest humans evolved from marine adapted primates.

Autarky to Patriarchy: If over the millennia one were to identify the primary social trend it would be toward a more *cooperative* society.

Cinderella survived the conflicts of household transition. The lesson is the value and power of *cooperative* society. Cinderella removes herself from the step-family with the help of her god-mother. Enchantment charms her prince.

In tribal society there were no step-families at life's banquet table. Both abundance and scarcity were shared. Profit-society *Takers* covet wealth at the top of the pyramid and relegate scarcity to those at the bottom.

Our only home is *change*: From big-bang to big-crunch, heat-energy expands as it cools. From energy *strings*, electrons, atoms, molecules, cells, animals, vegetables, minerals, and even people, all stuff is energy in perpetual *change*. Cosmos is *change*. Everything, all energy, and even people are subject to the cosmic laws of change.

Communal households: The Iroquois Federation had only one remedy for injuries; it was communal *gift-exchange*. An entire village must provide gifts to make amends. If a Huron is killed by another Huron, 30 gifts will suffice. But killing a woman requires 40 gifts since women are not easily replaced.

56-57 Venus Grottos de **Grimaldi** Earth Mother, 30,000 BC
58-Venus Dolní Věstonice, earliest ceramic 29,000 BC
http://en.wikipedia.org/wiki/Paleolithic_Venus

Killing a stranger requires more gifts as murders would deter trade and wars would arise too often. (Frank Goldsmith Speck, *The Iroquois, A Study in Cultural Evolution)*

Knowing an entire village is responsible was an adequate safeguard. As *communal property* includes land and material, theft is a rarity. Surplus food is shared. Long bark

87

houses belong to maternal clans, while tools, utensils, weapons, and *personal property* belong to the user.

59-60 Iroquois Longhouses early 30-40 person & 1885, 50-60 person;
http://en.wikipedia.org/wiki/Iroquois_longhouse#Iroquois_longhouse

In her introduction to *Origin of the Family*, Eleanor Leacock noted: in the early phases of human society all work and property were collective. People consumed what they produced directly. Land was communal property.

This situation persists in present communal societies. Speck, Leacock, and Lewis Henry Morgan mention the existence of a keen sense of democracy and equality in many tribal societies.

The Iroquois Federation was a model for Jefferson's draft of both *Declaration of Independence* and *Bill of Rights*.

Women's contribution: In terms of food, women were the backbone of communal tribal society. Women provided up to two-thirds of the food in Iroquois society. While men were the *meat-winners*, women were the *bread-winners*.

High protein diet appears to curb fertility, compared to low protein diet. High protein diet provides healthy kids, reducing the need or desire for more children. In this regard, the Iroquois diet provides some insight:

61-Hopi Earth Woman with clown pottery handle 1,000 AD

'They cultivate-gather: 15 maize (corn) varieties, 60 bean varieties, 8 native squash, 34 wild fruit, 11 nuts, 38 leaf-stem-bark foods, 12 edible roots, 6 fungi, 12 beverages, 11 plant infusions, and used maple sap as the sweeter for all. Also, there are 22 animal foods, 6 insects, and 4 mollusks.' (Frank Goldsmith Speck, *The Iroquois, A Study in Cultural Evolution*)

Due to their vital role, Iroquois women held major decision making power, appointing, and deposing male chiefs. Family did not exist independent of Iroquois society.

Husbands belong to one clan and wives belong to another. When marriages broke up, wives took their personal property and children back to her clan, as did husbands to his clan. Among North American tribes *mother-right* prevailed. Such values persist in most 21st Century families.

62-Courjeomet Earth Mother Marne, France 5,000 BC

Tribal communal values such as *mother-right* continue in all families. Family *nurture* is: 'give to each what's needed and each gives what they are able.'

Hutterite communities: Abolished private property and succeeded with little change for nearly 500 years. Living in *Christian communes,* they use modern technology. Pennsylvania German is the common language and global media-culture is shunned. Computer tech, higher education, and modern industrial production increasingly accompany high tech farming, and energy production. Hutterites created the kindergarten. In addition they have a German Bible school, Sunday school, and complete high schools.

Increasingly, they realize the need for higher education in farming and energy technology.

From an original population of 400 in the 1880's, over 100 Hutterite colonies total about 50,000 members. Their rate of increase is two to three times more than the rate for South Dakota; when a colony grows to 250 persons, a *daughter* colony branches off, similar to tribal groups.

63-Mother-child Hacilar, Turkey 5,000 BC

Hutterite success is thought to depend on strict adherence to the old German culture and Anabaptist religion of medieval Europe. While democratic in practice, the old patriarchal pattern continues in leadership. Work is communal. Women and men work as apprentices and in group labor. Hutterite marriage is rigidly monogamous and puritanical standards are maintained. First cousin marriage is denied, but second cousin and more removed kinship marriage is permitted. Birth control is taboo.
http://en.wikipedia.org/wiki/Hutterite

One can easily contrast communal societies with profit-society. While the Hutterites value people as a part of a larger spiritual community; profit-society values people as commodities to labor for the profit of a few.

12-HOUSEHOLD RELIGION: *Go into the garden and fetch me a pumpkin. Her godmother scooped out the inside, leaving nothing, but the rind and then touched it with her wand. 'I'll go and look at the rat trap,' said Cinderella, 'if there is a rat in it, we'll make a coachman of him.' 'You are right,' said her godmother, 'go and see.'*

(Charles Perrault, *Cinderella*, 1697)

Cinderella had knowledge of magic. She knew rats were needed. This her godmother affirmed. To succeed with her godmother, Cinderella had to be immersed in the old nature religion, but it was only one part of her life.

Cinderella's magic was more than a reaction to her suffering; it aided her struggle to be fully human. All aspects of society are reflected in its religion, culture, economy, and family structure. These are reflected in social structure. No one part of society can realistically be examined in isolation. Just as art mirrors society, religion reveals its soul.

Art, religion, and class: Profit-society art, religion, and culture reflect market values. Dehumanizing art reflects the dehumanization of society.

From ancient to modern times there persists an attempt to resist ruling class values. What begins as *Mystery* religion persists thru the ages, hidden in the cracks and recesses of civilization as *Natural* religion. It's no accident that *Cinderella* and most children's stories contain elements of the *Old Religion*.

Ostensibly children's stories support established values, but in fact teach mistrust of established values. It is less that women rediscover Natural religion; rather it is always present. Patriarchal abuse, torture, and murder are women's heritage; but the maternal power of women persists.

64-Burning Time 16th Century German pamphlet woodcut

The 2,500 year struggle between matriarchs' natural power and patriarchal rule persists. The life energy of motherhood, the eternal feminine, resists patriarchal lies, violence, and war.

Robert Graves' *The Greek Myths* treats myth as a reflection of ritualized mime in ancient religious rites. Myth serves as a vehicle for advancing the human spirit.

65-Witches' broomsticks 1440 AD earliest known drawing from
Le Champion des Dames by Martin le Franc

Greek myth reflects the struggle between matriarch fertility religion and patriarch Judean-Christian-Islamic sects.

Hearth religion: The relation between myth, religion, and household is stronger the further back one explores. The earliest center of human society is the *campfire*, likely the first human household. Campfire-hearth-household creates human society, culture, and religion.

Ancient Europe had no gods. The Great Goddess was regarded as immortal, changeless, and omnipotent. The concept of fatherhood had not been introduced into religious thought, prior to patriarch invasions, 2,000 BC.

The goddess took lovers, but for pleasure, not to provide children with a father. Men feared, adored, and obeyed the matriarch.

The hearth she tended was the earliest social center, and motherhood the prime mystery. The first victim of a Greek public sacrifice was always offered to Hestia of the hearth.

The hearth was also regarded as the sacrificial altar. Hestia represented personal security, happiness, motherhood, and the sacred duty of hospitality.
(Robert Graves, *The Greek Myths*)

66-Woman sacrificing to Hestia of the Hearth, Athens 600 BC

Knowing the relationship between coitus and child birth improved male status. Perhaps this knowledge was the first step in eroding the power of the queen-mother.

Early Greek myth is primarily concerned with changing relations between queen and lovers. Patriarchal conquest of Troy about 1,600 BC likely ended the wide-spread religious practice of male sacrifice. As described by Robert Graves in Homer's *Iliad*: Queens chose annual lovers from her male entourage for year-end mid-winter sacrifice.

This provided a symbol of fertility, rather than the object of her erotic pleasure. His sprinkled blood served to fructify trees, crops, and flocks. His flesh was eaten raw by the queen's fellow-nymph priestesses wearing the masks of bitches, mares, or sows. (Robert Graves, *The Greek Myths*)

Much of Greek myth is social-religious centered on the early tribal household, as the center of society. Hearth and household dominance continued until 500 BC and persists in many tribal societies.

The ancient people of the Mediterranean were a long way from the *affluent* societies of the equatorial rain forests. Matriarchal Pelasgians prior to 1,300 BC were primarily concerned with *survival*.

Fertility of land, animals, and people was the first concern. Just as one can easily conceive of a society such as our own in which money is the central concern, imagine a society focusing on fertility.

Mothers held power of fertility, for obvious reasons. With the consolidation of male power between 500-1000 BC, matriarchal influence began to fade. If there was a record of matriarchal society, it has largely disappeared, been subverted, destroyed, and buried by patriarchs. Victors write their own story. For 2,500 years, *His-story eclipses Her-story*. What remains is a tradition of myth.

Graves suggests Homer was the last of a matriarchal tradition of oral story telling. The *Iliad* and *Odyssey* are viewed as an effort of matriarchal advocacy in a society of encroaching male-rule.

Homer's epics devote considerable detail to the so-called heroes of Ionian, Dorian, and Achaean invading Aryans. Homer emphasized Aryan brutality, lust, cowardice, and stupidity. Odysseus is portrayed for his deceitfulness and deviousness rather than valor or intelligence.

Pelasgian household: Pre-Hellenic Greeks are known as Pelasgians. Pelasgians are thought to have migrated from Canaan in the Middle East about 10,000 years ago. Pelasgians were later dominated by Hellene, Ionian, Dorian, Achaean, Mycenaean, and Aeolian invaders from the Aryl-Ural Mountains of Eurasia.

67-Neolithic Mother Goddess, Menhir Brittany 2,500 BC;
68-Orphic Egg of Jacob Bryant (1774)
http://en.wikipedia.org/wiki/The_Greek_Myths

Robert Graves reconstructed the *Pelasgian creation myth* from supreme creator *Eurynome, Goddess of All Things*.

Eurynome arose naked from *Chaos*, parted sea from sky so she could dance upon the waves. Catching the north wind and, rubbing it between her hands, she warms the *pneuma*, wind generating the serpent *Ophion*, who mates with her.

In the form of a dove upon the waves, she lays the *Cosmic Egg* and bids *Ophion* to incubate it by coiling seven times around until it splits in two and hatches *all things that exist*, the sky, heavens, and all living creatures.
http://en.wikipedia.org/wiki/The_Greek_Myths

97

The key phrases in Graves' Pelasgian creation myth are:
1) *Goddess of all things* refers to women's social power;
2) *Divided sea from sky* is a unified concept of the Cosmos;
3) *Work of creation* refers to women creating all things of value, suggesting: What one creates, one must control.

Matriarchal suppression: By 1,200 BC Dorian suppression of women removed all magical powers except prophesy; reducing women to household slaves. Group marriage was replaced by Dorian-imposed monogamy.

Dorian conquests of goddess shrines were referred to as rapes of goddesses by Zeus. Rape continues as the ultimate form of terror against women. Little has changed since the Bronze Age. Dorian myth is replete with infidelities and conflicts between gods and goddesses. This may reflect Dorian family and political life.

Graves points this out quoting from the *Iliad*: Zeus and Hera bickered constantly. Vexed by his infidelities, she often humiliated him by her scheming ways. Though he would confide his secrets to her, and sometimes accept her advice, he never fully trusted Hera, and she knew that if offended beyond a certain point he would flog or even hurl a thunderbolt at her.

Great Goddess sacred fertility sex rites were ridiculed by the patriarchal Hellenes as adulterous and indecent.

Matriarchal society struggled to survive. There was a 1,500 year transition from matriarch to patriarch society.

Graves suggests hermaphrodites as one of the transitional religious concepts. *Hermaphroditus* was the sacred king deputizing for the queen, wearing artificial breasts as a badge of office. http://en.wikipedia.org/wiki/The_Greek_Myths

69-Votive Goddess blessing worshippers between
Beneficent household snakes, Athenian Agora 700 BC

Bronze Age Household: Patriarchal conquests caused changes in politics, religion, society, and in work patterns.

Some of the finest Cretan pots were made by women, and so originally were all the useful instruments invented by Athena: flute, trumpet, earthenware, plough, rake, ox-yolk, horse bridle, chariot, and ship; but in classical Hellenic Greece an artisan had to be a man. (Robert Graves, *The Greek Myths*)

Much of what is known about life in ancient societies such as division of work and the status of people is the result of observing, and recording burial objects.

Regarding British burial mounds, barrows of the same Bronze Age: Women in Bronze Age Britain were not slaves and held positions of trust and equality with men. Women were found interred apart from any male.

Women occupied important positions in the burial mounds, in some cases women were the sole tenant of a barrow. This is inconsistent with women's place in the home being merely a servile one.

The manufacture of pottery would be left to women, as was agriculture. Preparation of skins and sewing them into garments was the domain of women. This accounts for small bronze awls found with female skeletons. Cooking, children, and other tasks fully occupied a woman's day.
(Jacquetta Hawkes, *The World of the Past*)

Hellenic household transition: The Goddess fell by 1,000 BC. Women lost their power to Olympian invaders. Most destructive was the loss of women's power in the home by depriving them of their crafts. The patriarch victory was further defined by the conquering Hellenes:

In order to deprive women even further of their influence homosexual romance became a new pursuit as seen in the spread of Platonic ideas, about 500 BC. The intellectually dominant Greek woman was demeaned into the role of virtual household slave and child bearer.

The turnabout in power is reflected by the reversals in myth. Hecate is the original Triple-Goddess, supreme in heaven, on Earth and in Tartarus. But Hellenes emphasized her destructive powers at the expense of the creative until finally she was involved only in clandestine Mystery religion rites and black magic. (Robert Graves, *The Greek Myths*)

Women's resistance: Transition from matriarch to patriarch power was long and bloody spanning 1,500 years. In the early period resistance was well organized and effective. It took successive waves of invaders 1,500 years to subdue matriarch society.

The most effective matriarch defenders were the tribal Amazons. These were the Moon-Goddess's fighting priestesses. Amazon origins are attributed to Ukrainian Scythia, Turkish Anatolia, Crete, and Albania. During the period of resistance, 2,000 to 500 BC, Amazon rule was ferocious, total, and irresistible.

Amazon women fought and governed. Men were relegated to housework. To lessen the threat of male resistance, fighting priestesses cut leg tendons or crippled infant boys.

Amazons were the first to use cavalry and worked bronze for bows and shields shaped like half-moons. They made a fearsome spectacle in their bronze armor and animal skins.

70-Wounded Amazon of the Capitol, Rome,
71-Moon Goddess Gorgon Medusa Taranto, Italy 450 BC;
72-Amazon in trousers, shield, patterned cloth & quiver 470 BC,
73-Amazon mounted in Scythian garb 420 BC
http://en.wikipedia.org/wiki/Amazons

On an appointed day every spring, parties of young Amazons and young Gargarensians met at the summit of the mountain separating their lands and after performing joint sacrifice, spent two months together, enjoying intercourse under cover of night. As Amazons became pregnant, they returned home. Girl births were Amazons. Boys were sent to Gargarensians who distributed them among their huts. (Robert Graves, *The Greek Myths*)

Women's resistance to the destruction of their power involved: preservation of family-household; protecting social-religious life; and most important, armed resistance.

Amazons formed armies and adapted their society to life in armed, militarized mobile units to fight male invaders more effectively. Amazons used extreme measures: took no prisoners, castrated any man they met with a flint sickle, and raised only female children.

They recognized their desperate situation, declaring total war on male invaders. In the time of Theseus, Amazons invaded Athens and nearly destroyed the Mycenaean castle. (Helen Victry, *The Male Hierarchy*, from *Women Out of History* by Ann Forfreedom)

A similar resistance emerged throughout the land of the ancient Greek, Grakai, worshippers of the Grey Goddess. For hundreds of years the extremely conservative peasantry supported the matriarchy and the old religion, treating the invading Olympians as rebel upstarts.

Household sacrifice: In the *Iliad* the new kings declare, 'they are far better off than their fathers.' No doubt they were referring to the religious practice of male sacrifice.

To understand how opposition to matriarchy developed one need only note some of the matriarchal religious rites practiced through-out most of the Mediterranean up until 2,000 BC. In pre-Hellenic myth, the Goddess Nemesis picks the sacred king; and after all his seasonal transformations Nemesis opposes each with her own, finally devouring him at the summer solstice.

Hellenic myth reverses the parts. The goddess flees changing shape, but the king pursues and finally rapes her. After power passed to patriarchs, the murderous chase of the sacred king by the Goddess armed with a net was converted into a love chase of the Goddess by the sacred king. (Robert Graves, *The Greek Myths*)

The sacred king later becomes the devil, perverted by patriarchy, much as Judean-Christian-Islamic tradition evolves from matriarchy.

In the Oedipus cycle, the murder of his father Laius is the solar king's ritual death at the hands of his successor, the inter-regnum. The old solar king is thrown from a chariot and dragged by horses. Oak-kings fell beneath the double-axe and their bodies roasted in a bonfire.

The double-headed labrys axe, shaped like a waxing-waning moon joined back to back, symbolized creative-destructive goddess power.

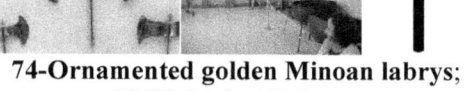

74-Ornamented golden Minoan labrys;
75-Eight-foot Labrys;
76-Labrys symbolizing pagan and women's movements
http://en.wikipedia.org/wiki/Labrys

Under the old system the new king, though a foreigner had in myth been a son of the old king whom he killed and whose widow he married. Later in the *Oedipus* cycle this is misrepresented as patricide and incest.

Similar to the Hindu Shiva-Kali cycle, these were part of a *death-creation cycle,* always celebrated as such. The practices were considered necessary to insure the cycle of

104

rebirth in the clan household. Household preservation was thought to depend on a series of sacrifices. Men as the least important household member were the logical sacrifice.

The *Oedipus* myth unifies both sacrifice and regeneration of tribal-clan household. The myth is probably the residue of religious rites with a basis in ancient events.

77-Astarte of Rhodes with leopards 650 BC

Çatalhöyük: is a large archeological site on the Anatolian plain of Turkey. The site is at least 10,000 years old and accommodated up to 10,000 people. Some suggest the agricultural revolution began at Çatalhöyük.

The site was composed entirely of domestic buildings, with no obvious public buildings. People lived in attached mud-brick houses resembling Pueblo/Clovis dwellings arranged in a clustered honeycomb maze. There were no footpaths or streets. Access was by holes in the ceiling, with doors reached by ladders and stairs.

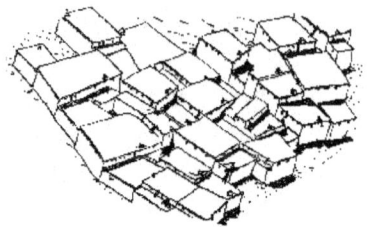

78-Çatalhöyük *town,* http://en.wikipedia.org/wiki/Çatalhöyük

Rooftops were effectively streets, as is still the case in much of the Middle East. Ceiling openings served as ventilation, allowing smoke from open hearths and ovens to escape. Vivid murals and figurines were found throughout the settlement on interior and exterior walls. Distinctive clay figurines of women were found, notably the Seated Woman of Çatalhöyük, below.

79-Seated Woman with lions, http://en.wikipedia.org/wiki/Çatalhöyük

Graves, murals, and figurines suggest Çatalhöyük had a religion rich in symbols. Rooms appear to be religious shrines or public meeting areas. Images include: voluptuous pregnant women, auroch horns, leopards, lions, vultures, men's erect phalluses, and stag hunting scenes. Figures of women and men are about equal.

Golden Age: The earliest period of Pelasgian society is referred to as the Golden Age myth: 'People lived without cares or labor, eating only acorns, wild fruit, and honey dripping from trees, drinking sheep and goat milk, never growing old, dancing and laughing much; death to them was no more terrible than sleep.' (Robert Graves, *The Greek Myths*)

The myth of the Golden Age suggests Bee Goddess rule. A Silver Age and a silver race are described as the metal of the Moon Goddess and matriarchy. Men were still despised and agriculture was introduced along with occasional wars.

The earliest Hellenic Indo-European invaders comprise a third race of Bronze Age herders. The 8th Century BC Greek poet Hesiod wrote in his *Works and Days*, dividing history into five ages. He referred to a Bronze and Iron Age: (Robert Graves, *The Greek Myths*)

Then Zeus the Father again made humankind,
A breed of bronze, far differently designed,
A breed from the ash-tree sprung, huge-limbed and dread,
Lovers of battle and horror, no eaters of bread
Their hearts were hard, their adamant hearts: none stood
To meet their power of limbs and their hardihood

And the swing of the terrible arms their shoulders bore.
Bronze were their arms, bronze the armor they wore,
And their tools; for no dark iron supplied their needs.

Çatalhöyük Golden Age: While Çatalhöyük digs are far from complete, settlement at the site is at least 10,000 years old. It was a Neolithic center for flint, obsidian, metal tools, ornaments, jewelry, and farm implements.

Artifacts show evidence of: large-scale weaving, wood working, pottery, bone carving, wheat, barley, fruit, vegetables, large-scale grain storage, and bread baking.

Other activities included baking stones for sling-shots, wood cutting, weaving mats and baskets, bead drilling, wool spinning, copper and lead smelting, pigment making, wall painting, sculpture, and hide curing.

It was a well-rounded manufacturing, agriculture, and religious center. Çatalhöyük may well be the source of later Aegean civilizations, much as 11,000 year old Jericho was a Middle East hub. http://en.wikipedia.org/wiki/Jericho

Perhaps most remarkable is the lack of evidence of violence or animal sacrifice at Çatalhöyük: There are no signs of violent death or skull trephining. A few show broken limbs, arthritis, and caries.

On the whole dentition is excellent. Childbirth, fevers, and pneumonia may be primary causes of death, not degenerative diseases. Bones of women and children far outnumber men, suggesting childbirth as a major cause of death. (James Mellaart, Çatalhöyük a Neolithic Town in Anatolia)

Among the symbols found at Çatalhöyük are the use of red and black in wall paintings to represent life and death. West walls tend to be painted in red and east walls in black. One wall painting seemed to represent a honey comb with eggs or chrysalises on boughs and with bees.

80-Çatalhöyük Vulture-Auroch horn shrine

This is similar to beehive symbols appearing later in Pelasgian Greece. Alternate red and black lined paintings with a net design may represent regeneration and death phases of life. Nets may symbolize sacrificial net garments such as Clytemnestra used to kill Agamemnon, or the fiery net made by Medea to punish Jason's concubine.

There are many depictions of: black bulls and vultures, net patterns, horns, crosses, labrys, and four-petal flowers decorating walls and statuettes. These appear to represent fertility-death and creation-destruction-regeneration. All

these symbols were widely used in later Greek society.
(James Mellaart, Çatalhöyük a Neolithic Town in Anatolia)

The Goddess is seen representing fertility, life, and the hunt. Frequent links between the Goddess and wild animals provide evidence for this view. Many graphics of Astarte with wild animals in this book suggest the Goddess as huntress, with dominion over all animals, and life.

Of special interest is a statuette of a mother giving birth in a grain-bin shrine. Floral patterns and textile designs indicate her role as a weaver. Wall paintings of vultures feeding on the dead, and giving birth to a son in the form of a bull suggest her role as Goddess of life and death.

In Neolithic times the divine family consisted of four aspects; in order of importance these are: mother, daughter, son, and father. The primary deity was the Great Mother. A lesser deity was her mate or son. This concept of the divine family is confirmed in later Bronze Age Greece.

Other than breasts, pregnant figures, and occasional phallus, no other sex organs were found. Male influence in later cultures is indicated by prominent display of primary sex organs. The frequent show of horns may suggest the male phallus; but the double curved horns could just as well indicate vulva and uterine horns, a horse-shoe omega, Ω.

Çatalhöyük artifacts suggest abundance, fertility, and increase associated with women as the source of life. It

110

may then be seen how a *household fertility religion* arises based on conserving and increasing all life.

Mystery religion, based on the hearth-fire, grew into rites involving cycles of birth, life, death, and resurrection. Creation myth is based on the reproductive power of the eternal feminine. In the beginning, women were empowered by their control over their own fertility. Matriarchy is mother rule.

Patriarchy could only control society by subverting household, family, women, and especially mother-child. Social-economic power begins and ends in the family household.

In the 21ˢᵗ Century, violence and war result in the global decline of civilization. Much of the decline can be attributed to male power fragmenting the family household.

Typically, academics deny the existence of matriarchy. *Male-rule* can be made more acceptable and appear natural if it is shown *mother-rule* and egalitarian societies never existed. Archeology confounds this view.

Promoting the notion of male-rule is akin to promoting the idea of a master-race. Too many contradictions keep surfacing. What began as a matriarchal myth of the first *man born from a woman's rib* later becomes the patriarchal story of a *woman born from a man's rib*.

81-BrassempouyVenus, ivory 20,000 BC,
http://en.wikipedia.org/wiki/Venus_figurines

Roots of Matriarchy: There is substantial data supporting matriarchal fertility values:

1) The oldest sculptured head is shown above. These women fertility heads are found from Aq Kupruk in northern Afghanistan to Moravia, Czech Republic, and Brassempouy, France. (Louis Dupree, *Face from 20,000 BC*)

2) The Çatalhöyük Great Goddess of Anatolia Turkey may be older than 10,000 years. Archeologist James Mallart considered this site a matriarchal, religious, farming, and manufacturing town.

82-Cycladic marble votive 1.5 m largest known 2,800-2,300 BC
http://en.wikipedia.org/wiki/Cycladic_civilization

112

3) The Greek Pelasgian period from 2,000-700 BC was characterized by female fertility votives; as was the earlier Cycladic Greek Aegean Sea culture of 3,200-2,000 BC. During the Cyclades period most sculptures were flat fertility figures with pointed legs to stick in grain bins.
http://en.wikipedia.org/wiki/Pelasgians & http://en.wikipedia.org/wiki/Cyclades

4) At Çatalhöyük, fertility artifacts were household objects. Hearths, campfires, and cooking cauldrons symbolize bee hives and pregnancy. Breasts, buttocks, and pregnant forms are most prevalent.

5) Queen-mother household initiates family, clan, and tribe. Breasts were recognized as food sources for infants. Large breasts in most Venus figures represent nurturing abundance in the mother-child household. It's suggested, *'Mother and child constitute the first household.'*

83-Rangda the Bali, Java, and Thai witch widow 1,000 BC
Symbolic of the eternal battle between good and evil
http://en.wikipedia.org/wiki/Rangda

6) *Hestia* of the Hearth requires elaborate purification rites before hearth sacrifice. Sanitation and nurturing are vital

113

aspects of hearth religion. Hearth and kitchen are the household centers. Some religions continue to burn ritual candles in the kitchen.

13-ABUNDANCE and SCARCITY: *All the women carefully studied her appearance in every detail, with the intention of dressing in the same way themselves, if such materials and clever dress makers could be found.* (Charles Perrault, *Cinderella*, 1697)
Society is shaped by abundance or scarcity, influenced by both nature and people. *Cinderella* provides a parable in the form of a stressful and abusive step-family.

The *social-effect* amounts to shaping Cinderella into a household servant. Early merchant society creates the *class* system of the mistress, master, and servant, as well as craft apprentice, journeyman, and master. Cinderella's *nuclear* family internalizes the *class* struggle between master, mistress, and servant.

The loss of Cinderella's mother would be less traumatic in larger families with multiple adult women. Isolation and loneliness exist in smaller *nuclear* families with more work to do and fewer people to do it. This is a familiar story. Cinderella is the household drudge doing the housework so the step-family can step up the social *class* ladder.

With abundance there is little reason to fabricate a *class*-society. Iroquois and Hutterite are classless societies sharing abundance, work, resources, and spiritual values.

114

The social-effect of *class* depends on scarcity. When less is available the social-effect is to accumulate and dole-out based on status. In ancient society, the wealthy and their police apparatus own most resources. This arrangement has not significantly changed over the millennia.

Families continue to share resources, providing for needs. *Class* structure is based primarily on the concentration of wealth. This is the basic control mechanism of male rule, as evidenced by looking at the U.S. budget. The fastest increase in expenditures is interest payments. Interest and debt is owned by the financial sector of the economy.
http://en.wikipedia.org/wiki/U.S._budget_deficit

Interest is only one factor in the rapid amassing of wealth. Regardless of business success or failure, there is usually interest and debt, especially in home mortgages.

Finance and banking are the major global source of interest debt. To understand why one out of 10,000 families controls global wealth, one need only examine U.S. banking-finance. In 1947 financial industry profits were only 10% of total profits. By 2010 it grew to 50%.
http://en.wikipedia.org/wiki/Financial_industry

Globally, an estimated $64 trillion is owned by 1,645 billionaires and 13 million millionaires in 2014. These are super-rich *Haves*, mostly old white men.

Haves comprise less than 0.2% of the global population (13 million out of 7,000 million). Total global 2014 Gross

115

Domestic Product, GDP, is estimated at $102 trillion. Billionaire-millionaire wealth accounts for 63% of total global wealth. http://en.wikipedia.org/wiki/Global_economy, and http://en.wikipedia.org/wiki/Billionaire, http://en.wikipedia.org/wiki/Millionaire,

The *social effect* of hoarded wealth retards human development and *family functions* by:
1) Shrinking family *income*;
2) Reducing *births* of wageworkers, and houseworkers;
3) *Less buying* means less *Have* wealth; the bottom line is
4) 99.8% of *Have-not* labor *produces* the 0.2% of *Haves*.

Leisure-Time: Time spent recuperating from work is considered *leisure-time*. In this regard, leisure is part of the work process; just as sleep is part of the life process.

More accurately *leisure* is a form of *recreation*, in the existential sense of the word. The word *recreation* refers to *re-creation* of the body. Time spent in *recreation*, leisure, and even sleep maintains, rebuilds, and *re-creates* us. In this regard *recreation* is also housework.

Prior to the market economy, people did not differentiate between *work-time* and *leisure-time*. While most work requires *breaks, leisure-time* is considered the time spent before and after wagework.

Housework, wagework, income, and *leisure* create *commodities, shopping* and *buying.* These fuel the profit-

116

system *Haves*. Leisure, as with rest and sleep, provides energy renewal for the next work shift. *Leisure-time* uses *income* for *shopping* and *buying*.

The major housework activity is *shopping*. Increasingly, *shopping* is viewed as *recreation*. *Shopping* is part of house work, transforming *income* and human *energy* into purchases for family renewal.

In ancient times our ancestors *hunted* and *gathered*. Now we *gather* coupons and *hunt* for bargains. In earlier eras mothers might have said, 'Don't come home without red meat.' Now they say, 'Don't come home without a job.'

We are *educated* and *socialized* to accept our role in the family and the economy; then we become units of *labor*. We are *plugged* into profit-economy *sockets*, as if we are energizing electric *plugs*.

Human value is quantified in terms of income, productivity, and consumption. People are quantified as producers and consumers. Our value as *people* is transformed into *tools* for increasing *profit*. Market technology transforms human *quality* into *quantity*.

As with Cinderella, family and household are transformed into profit-system tools.

The Good-Life: Most societies have a concept of the *good-life*. The *good-life* reflects belonging to family, clan, tribe, or nation and is most relevant in affluent societies. In most societies, people believe they lead the *good-life*.

Satisfying human needs and socializing are the main values of the *good-life*. At university we often joked about the *good-life*. For students the *good-life* is sex, diplomas, good jobs, high status, and plenty of money.

In affluent tribal societies, the *good-life* is health and meeting the needs of: family, household, clan, and tribe. The *good-life* is also hope for the future.

Tribal societies define the *good-life* as: day-long festivals, ritual, ceremony, contests, games, hunting, gathering, and observing totem-taboo. **The *good-life* is socializing**.

For most cultures, *socializing* is primary. The *good-life* includes the *glittering prizes* of good fortune, and is more a matter of *status* than material gain. Included are honor, social *status,* prestige, and coming of age *trophies*.

Marketplace social effects: Discrimination reduces family income and *splits families* to increase market consumption. To increase profits and reduce costs, the profit-system divides people on the basis of sex, race, ethnicity, religion, education, and age.

Filling-out Internet job applications and going to interviews reveal the effects of recent anti-discrimination laws concerning *age, sex, and race*. At the end of job applications there are optional references to qualifying as: a

118

veteran, on public assistance, disability, mixed race, as well as other *favored* status. These are *favored* qualifications as tax benefits may be gained by employers hiring people in these categories.

Joel Roche's *Confessions of a Househusband* noted the *social effect* of home-isolation. Separation from the outside world isolates houseworkers and stifles human feelings.

The feeling of household isolation, *house arrest*, becomes laziness, selfishness, and callousness. Sex-role privilege inflicts enormous damage on men, turning half of humanity into subordinates and the other half into rivals, isolating and making fear and loneliness the norm of existence.

(Joel Roche, Confessions of a househusband, Ms Magazine)

Casualty nation: Household isolation affects everyone. The profit-system segregates by income, race, sex, religion, age, health, and ethnicity. We tend to view each other more as competitors than people.

Discrimination stems from *educating-socializing* children to think of *others* as stereotypes. We are *conditioned* to ask, 'What can they do for me?' Women are *socialized* to view men as income *providers*. Men view women as sex, family, and housework providers. Men learn to see women as an assortment of body parts.

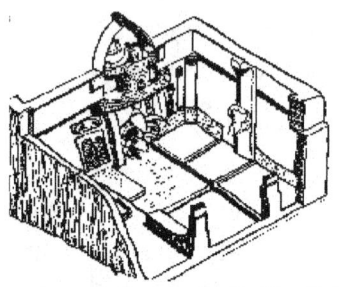

84-Birth Shrine Auroch horns-skulls Çatalhöyük 6,500 BC

Many couples grow beyond the sex; but the growth is on a faulty foundation. It's why a mature relationship crumbles and the old sex roles come exploding off the block like sprinters. (Jack Litewka, 'The Socialized Penis,' *Liberation*)

Reification: is transforming people into *things*, sorted into groups of workers, buyers, and sellers. This semi-conscious action deprives people of their humanity. It's far easier to control *things* than *people*.

As the profit system exerts pressures that are hard to resist, both mental and physical freedom are diminish. By restricting people to household drudgery, with costly access to childcare and assistance, the houseworker becomes a prisoner of the household. In *profit-society,* houseworkers and wageworkers are transformed into *things*.

120

The most destructive result of the global *profit-economy* is the reduction of family *income*. Part of the destruction is the isolation and competition fostered by the *profit-system*.

The parent-child *nuclear* family focuses, increases, and transmits social-economic stress to the people inside and outside the family. *Nuclear* families magnify divisiveness.

Market media persuade men to view themselves as sexual and economic rivals. At the same time women are increasingly victimized and resistant to the oppression and respond in kind at every opportunity. Much of women's resistance is based on their sexual power. Even when sex is a free choice, women and men pay dearly.

When sex is coerced or forced, women increasingly resort to legal action. Male power loss plays out as rape—an angry effort to gain power over women.

The growing imbalance of wealth also indicates the accumulation of power by super-rich white men. The vast majority of people increasingly suffers loss of income, loss of control over their lives, and increased anxiety. Global wealth grows along with anxiety, violence, and war.

The current state of global decay convinces people that government exists to serve super-rich white men. One politician had the gall to say, 'If the poor paid us more than the rich, we would serve the poor.'

We are both *victims* and *victimizers* to the extent we *hide-out* and remain passive. Increasingly, families suffering the inequities of hoarded wealth and power, take their frustrations out on each other. The number of divorces now equal marriages. http://www.divorcestatistics.org/

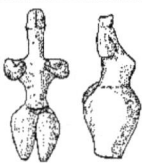

85 & 86-Neolithic fertility figures, Macedonia 6,000 BC

Larger families often have more wage earners. Smaller families feel the stress of needing multiple part-time jobs. Recently, a woman with four part-time jobs died in her car. She was trying to sleep between jobs. 'Dunkin' Donuts Worker's Death Reveals True Cost of Our Low-Wage, Part-Time Economy,' *the Huffington Post*, 08/29/2014

Lower wages and higher prices hit women hard, adding to a *growing problem* of women in low-wage jobs. Women make up two-thirds of low-wage workers. Over the last five years, 35% of women's job gains were in low-wage sectors, compared to 18% percent for men.

Women suffer more than men as there are 3.3 million U.S. women in multiple jobs, compared to 3.4 million men. Statistics note women spend 88% of a day at *housework*.

For *wagework* the ratio is 12% for women and 20% for men. http://www.bls.gov/news.release/atus.t01.htm

87-Mother and child Hacilar, Turkey 5,600 BC

14-LYSISTRATA: *It's hard for women, you know, to get away. There's so much to do: Husbands to be patted and put in good tempers. So fine, it comes to this—Greece saved by women! Our country's fate is henceforth in our hands.* (From Aristophanes' *Lysistrata*)
These are the very ornaments of the rescue.
These crocus gowns, this outlay of the best myrrh, slippers, and
Cosmetics dusting beauty, robes with rippling creases of light.
O women, if we would compel the men to bow to peace,
We must refrain from every depth of love.
Our bodies burning naked through the folds,
With our dear Venus-plats plucked trim and neat.
Their stirring love will rise up furiously,
They'll beg our arms to open. That's our time!
We'll disregard their knocking, beat them off—
And they will soon be rabid for a Peace.
I'm sure of it. (Aristophanes, *Lysistrata,* Athens 411 BC)

It's not known what Aristophanes had in mind when writing *Lysistrata*. In any case the message still rings true. The power of this ancient drama is easier to grasp if alternate interpretations are considered.

123

First, the meaning should be viewed in terms of Aristophanes' other plays such as *Birds*, *Frogs*, *Clouds*, and *Knights*, as political satire built around a formula.

88-Lysistrata, Aubrey Beardsley 1896, http://en.wikipedia.org/wiki/Lysistrata

Lysistrata is an earthy commentary on the follies of the Peloponnesian Wars, 431-404 BC. Aristophanes wrote Lysistrata in 411 BC, expressing the popular disgust and frustration of Athenians with the interminable war.

Patriarchal invaders dominated the heights of Mount Olympus and cities such as Athens. However the peasantry, and probably Aristophanes, remained conservative in defense of Matriarchy and feminine deities.

Second, the play is largely an exploitative erotic farce with little attempt at realism. If this was the case then the play was an effort at ridiculing the war and those who stubbornly supported it.

Third, the drama was a vehicle for mythic truths that combined sensuality and buffoonery, with insights into the nature of the human condition. The power of Hellenic

124

patriarchy subverting the once powerful matriarchy is another issue of that time. These views support each other.

Certainly Lysistrata serves as an ideal model for illuminating some key concepts:
1) Lysistrata dramatizes women's residual *social power*.
2) The drama demonstrates how women can focus and magnify their demands into *radical action*.
3) Lysistrata acts to overcome an oppressive war, by exercising *matriarchal* leadership.
4) Most important is the demonstration that radical action need *not involve violence*.
5) Purposeful comedy shows the *sexual* power of women. Lysistrata plans the strategy and tactics of resistance. The sex-rebellion is unexpected, causing surprise and shock.
6) The *weapons* of resistance are hiding in plain sight as the clothing, cosmetics, and the other tools of feminine power.

Women's power has always been based on controlling sex. Matriarchal power, for thousands of years before the patriarchal conquests, was based on producing and nurturing people in the household.

The matriarchal period, prior to 500 BC, largely depended on women's tribal power; specifically control of fertility *magic*. Fertility is the *power to increase*. It includes most household chores. Household fertility encompasses the crafts of pottery, food production, gathering, preservation, and storage; as well as weaving, fruit, vegetable, human, and animal increase.

89-Athena "reborn" from the head of Zeus;
Childbirth goddess Metis as Eileithyia, right, assists 550–525 BC
http://en.wikipedia.org/wiki/Greek_mythology

The above depiction of Athena reborn from the head of Zeus is symbolic of Hellenic patriarchy consolidating power. It's significant that patriarchy depicts a male god birthing a female goddess; suggesting fertility-reproductive power is sufficiently important to remove from women.

To the mind of the conservative native population this likely appeared as a ridiculous farce. It was and remains indelibly etched on the human psyche that only females bear offspring. The hubris of conquering patriarchs could not eclipse the reality of matriarchy. This is why Aristophanes ridiculed Hellenic *upstarts* in his comic dramas. Ridicule is the velvet glove of resistance.

Seeds of conflict: No matter how well entrenched a social system, elements of conflict always remain. If the Greek classics tell us anything, it is that every social system contains the seeds of its own destruction. Just as matriarchs were violently subverted, father-rule self-destructs from the fall-out of its own greed and violence.

Lysistrata's message is: Women are not only human beings, with voices and rights equal to men; but women are the source of human existence. The sexual power of women can insure a bright future, or bring about the opposite.

Fewer marriages and births, along with increasing divorce and family break-up, result from economic down-turns.

No matter how bleak the prospects, women know they control the future. The creative power of women appears in the form of their struggle.

The majority of low-income women acquire most of their own daily household necessities. Women are unavoidably involved in the *grey-market* economy. They depend on their own market enterprise for income. This is also the case wherever family income falls short.

In Africa they are referred to as *Market Women*. Globally, low-income women create markets for surplus-second hand goods and services.

Poor women of the Americas are dynamic, decisive, and are continually devising household strategies. Often women-centered households are unstable unions. To survive, women find it necessity to mate serially with a number of men. Having serial mates is a major way of coping with poverty.

Serial-mating is an innovative and dynamic method of dealing with poverty. It provides women with a better existence than the single-mate pattern could under the same circumstances. (Rayna R. Reiter, *Toward an Anthropology of Women*)

When a Latin woman marries, she is subject to her husband's whims. The husband has access to his wife's resources as well as his own. One woman explained:

'I would rather not marry the man. If I marry I will not be free to move about and find the work I choose; he would have control over the money I earn. If he fails to provide for me and my children or if he abuses me; turns gallero and spends all his money on cockfights, women, and alcohol I will leave him. I'd leave the kids with my mother and go to Santo Domingo to work.' (Judith K. Brown, *Toward an Anthropology of Women*)

It's the poorest women who are forced into this pattern. But even amongst poor and middle class women of the Americas a similar pattern emerges.

The disruptive pattern of the profit-economy becomes a major factor in family break-ups. The cost of maintaining multiple households, together with low wages, force continual change in family structure.

90-Taoist Kuan Yin mother and child 1,000 BC
91-Guanyin & child, Chinese Madonna and Child
http://en.wikipedia.org/wiki/Guanyin

Serial-mating, cooperative, and communal life is an attempt at living with profit-system abuse.

15-WHAT'S TO BE DONE? *He made Cinderella sit down and hold out her foot; the little slipper went on easily and fitted perfectly as if it had been molded to her foot in wax.* (Charles Perrault, *Cinderella*, 1697)
From ancient to current times the human household reshapes itself in response to environmental change.

Over the last three-million years of multiple cataclysms and *die-offs,* humanity evolved from a global low-point of a few thousand, after the deluge 13,000 years ago, to seven-billion in 2014. Holocene extinction included the disappearance of mega-fauna mammals, starting about 13,000 years ago with the end of the last Ice Age.
http://en.wikipedia.org/wiki/Holocene_extinction

129

92-Pregnant fertility shrine Çatalhöyük 6,500 BC

The last five-million years of primate evolution witnessed primate *hordes* and *bands* transform into human clans, tribes, and family-households. It's suggested that *nuclear* families result from man-made *scarcity*, rather than environmental disasters, as in the past. Some view the impending global crisis as a result of a world devouring profit-system. Others view the destructive profit-system as an opportunity for reinventing humanity.

In the last 2,500 years, *patriarch-authority* depended on property, government, religion, nuclear family, and men. Property and profit are patriarchal inventions.
    Matriarch-stewardship starts with mothers, family, clan, and tribe. After each *crisis* mothers take charge, reproduce, and rebuild the human family. **Women invent society.**

A worst (or best?) case scenario leaves Earth, cleansed of people and open to microbes such as Cyano-bacteria blue green algae. Cyano are a likely *back-up* for life on Earth.

130

93-Athena Mycenae mother of invention 625 BC
(National Archaeological Museum of Athens) http://en.wikipedia.org/wiki/Athena

Cyano took charge of evolution over the last 3.5-billion years. It took billions of years to generate enough oxygen to support complex life. One candidate for Earth-renewal is Cyano. Here's the reasoning: http://en.wikipedia.org/wiki/Cyanobacteria

1) Cyano was first to use sunlight, water, and carbon dioxide to *photosynthesize* their own food and fill Earth's atmosphere with their waste product, *oxygen*;

2) Cyano is the most *beneficial* life form populating Earth over its five-billion year existence;

3) Cyano is *resilient* and *prolific*; probably exceeding the grains of sand on Earth, and the stars in the sky;

4) Cyano inhabits *every niche* on Earth, and likely proliferates throughout the Cosmos;

5) Cyano is found *everywhere*: miles below the Earth, in soil, within rock crevasses, in oceans, in plants, animals, living in clouds, and in the atmosphere;

6) Cyano is literally *manna* from heaven, arriving on comets, meteors, and other space stuff;

7) Cyano provides excellent *nutrition* of protein, fat, carbs, vitamins, and minerals; Cyano are consumed globally as spirulina. http://en.wikipedia.org/wiki/Spirulina_(dietary_supplement)

New objectives: Reinventing humanity is an on-going process, with or without cataclysms or die-offs. It is no accident that women and mothers play a major part in Biotechnology and Genetic professions.

Mothers' intimacy with birthing, child nurturing and family provide instinctual motivation for women in the genotech fields. Concern with the Earth must be sufficiently broad to deal with the global environment, as well as social-economic issues.

People only raise questions that can be answered. In this regard social-economic problems raise questions about the broader human condition. The questions raised and answered reflect evolving ideas about humane solutions extending beyond the needs of people. The network of all life on planet Earth requires the same concern as do people.

It's increasingly evident that the geometric increase in the human population threatens life on Earth and people in particular. It's argued that global fertility will fall below replacement rates in the 2020s; and world population will peak below 9-billion by 2050, followed by a long decline—

if you believe. https://www.project-syndicate.org/commentary/the-end-of-population-growth

The great flood was the last global die-off 13,000 years ago. The main cause was global warming, along with tectonic-plate shifts and polar magnetic reversal. The agricultural revolution some 10,000 years ago began with perhaps 100,000 people.

Since that time increased food production has been followed by exponential population increases. About 4,000 years ago, climate change began to drive northern Indo-European herders south into the Middle East, Mediterranean, and Aegean regions.

Ural-Aral Mountain migrants were at first assimilated into indigenous matriarchal tribes. Later groups invaded. The battle of the sexes had begun. As patriarchal power grew, so did violence, war, and population. From the 100 million at the start of the Latin-Roman city-states 3,000 years ago, and the 200 million population 2,000 years ago, global population reached the first billion by 1800. http://en.wikipedia.org/wiki/Population_growth

Patriarch power came into its own with global merchant trade and the industrial revolution over the last 400 years. In the 1800s merchants, corporations, and bankers began to understand the relationship between growing population, wagework, consumption, and profit.

Corporate-banking competition soon led to consortiums, cartels, trusts, monopolies, and oligarchs. Oligarchs are now global hoarders of a vast amount of wealth and power.

Democratic principles of sharing and distribution of wealth is considered by oligarchs as *unworkable*. Oligarchs strive to keep it unworkable. Instead they lobby for tax-reducing charity, welfare, and government handouts for themselves.

Many of the *profit-hungry* are unwilling to compete on equal terms. They are *herd* animals with instincts to follow the latest profit-fashion, even if it leads the herd over an economic cliff, as is now the case.

This is especially true of cost-cutting. Since the 1970s cost-cutting resulted in transforming full-time to part-time work, cutting work hours, wages, income, and leading to less buying. The persistent global down-turn reflects this.

While a few hundred billionaire oligarchs become wealthier and more powerful, the global economy implodes as income, consumption and the global economy spiral downward. U.S. average wages are down 7% over the last 40 years, while commodity prices have increased ten-fold.

Wage stagnation and rising inequality as the wealth of the *Haves* increases is far from a normal market economy. It is bogus capitalism by lobbyists and media of the super-rich oligarchs, distorting markets and exploiting the Earth.

The alphabet soup of *security* agencies is already in control. The U.S. *security* apparatus is the fastest growing sector of the economy. That should tell us something. Which is the bigger threat, the growing police-state here at home, or the religious lunatics financed by global oligarchs?

Something similar occurred at the end of the Soviet era. The secret police captured the Russian government, and the nation's wealth. The head of the KGB was Putin and now he controls Russia. Is the U.S. heading in the same direction or have we already arrived?

Boiling a frog: Daniel Quinn's *The Story of B* provides a summary of the global problem:

If a frog is placed in luke-warm water it will remain quietly. Heat the water slowly and the frog will go into a stupor, similar to a person in a warm bath. Continued gradual heating and the frog will contentedly allow itself to be boiled to death.

The cauldron of European civilization began to heat as Ural-Aral-Aryan *Kurgan Waves* invaded from the Mountains of Eurasia. The Kurgans, a herding migratory people, domesticated horses and perfected the use of chariots. They migrated from 6,000 to 3,500 years ago.

Kurgan migrations were essentially hostile military incursions. A new Bronze-age warrior culture imposed itself on relatively peaceful Greek *matriarch* culture. Patriarch warriors replaced matriarchs. It was Bronze-age warriors who fortified settlements and built hill-forts.

In the Americas a similar scenario unfolded with the decimation of Native Americans at the hands of Europeans. http://en.wikipedia.org/wiki/Kurgan_hypothesis

The Middle East *cauldron* 10,000 years ago began a slow *heating* with the gradual growth of agriculture and population. In the 21st Century it reaches the *boiling* point.

More people require more grain and growing more grain results in more people. The *production-population* feed-back loop continues. In most cases, abundance of food and resources precedes population growth.

For 6,000 years, prior to Kurgan waves, Europe and the Middle East, like the contented frog, enjoyed the slow heating of the cultural cauldron. Sun-dried bricks, pottery wheel, kiln, textiles, and plow, provided significant advances. http://en.wikipedia.org/wiki/Ancient_Greek_technology

What brought the water to the *boil* was not agriculture, but grain cultivation to the max—*totalitarian* agriculture. Patriarch rule commanded: 'be fruitful and multiply; *farm to the max; take all land; and oppose all competition.* This defines *totalitarian* agriculture.

Every calorie study shows: the more food that comes from farming the harder you have to work for it. Famine is

136

never found apart from agriculture. Hunter-gatherers rarely starve. Starvation and famine are products of agriculture.

94-Lilith, Ishtar, Ereshkigal, Babylonia 2,000 BC
Owls later represent Athena, http://en.wikipedia.org/wiki/Lilith

Sumerian agriculture preceded Babylonian by 2,000 years. Sumer patriarchy forbade matriarch polyandry, a custom of women marrying multiple men. http://en.wikipedia.org/wiki/Sumer

Fraternal polyandry was traditionally practiced among Tibetans in Nepal, parts of China and part of northern India, in which two or more brothers are married to the same wife, with the wife having equal sexual access to the brothers. *Fraternal polyandry* is most common in egalitarian society with high male mortality or absenteeism.

Conquest of Mesopotamia was completed by Hammurabi 4,000 years ago, requiring intensive farming to support workers and armies. http://en.wikipedia.org/wiki/Babylonia

95-Draupadi & 5 Pandavas husbands; wife Draupadi is far right.
Deogarh, Dasavatar temple. http://en.wikipedia.org/wiki/Polyandry

The Middle East was heating-up. *Totalitarian* agriculture resulted in constant war with neighboring city-states. It was a religious zeal that dictated: *'All the food in the world belongs to us, without limit. Hunt-down our enemies, competitors—destroy them and their access to food.'*

As agriculture and population grew so did fear. Fear is the ideology of *Haves*—even into the 21st Century.

Over the last two hundred years the profit-economy pursued a policy of maximum *market expansion. Haves* reduce family income, resulting in falling *consumption*, marriage, and the birth of new consumers. In the 21st Century the waters are starting to *boil*. Humanity is on the *boil* with endless wars, violence, terrorism, economic exploitation, increasing suicides, reduced births, and destruction of the global middle class. The profit-economy cash-cow is dying.

138

Hopes and fears: There is a growing awareness that our *grab-and-take* culture is on the *boil*. Like frogs in a stupor of gradual heating, our leaders are locked in a stupor of mindless exploitation.

It's hard to throw-off a culture of *expansion-to-the-max*. It began on the Tigris-Euphrates 6,000 years ago with food and population expansion chasing each other. The slow heating is now a *boil*. It's a global metastasis forced on the Earth by a few hundred white men in lock-step, following the leader over the cliff of global catastrophe.

There is hope. *Green* political parties are now active in 100 countries: *Greens* advocate social justice, nonviolence, and Earth stewardship, as opposed to global exploitation. *Greens* believe these issues lead to world peace. A *Greens* Charter lists six guiding principles: ecological wisdom, social justice, participatory democracy, nonviolence, sustainability, and respect for diversity.'

Greens maintain an alliance with the *European Free Alliance* of stateless nations such as *Welsh Plaid Cymru* and the *Scottish National Party*. *Greens* and *European Free Alliance* have 58 seats in the European Parliament. It is now the fourth largest party in the European Parliament.
http://en.wikipedia.org/wiki/Green_party

Since the 1970s, *Green* thinking has significantly influenced a new generation. Except in the U.S., higher

139

education is freely available in most developed nations fostering progressive and *Green* attitudes.

Together with Green global media, especially the Internet, a new progressive constituency is emerging to replace the moribund establishment and moderate the heat under the cauldron of civilization.

16-DO WE HAVE A FUTURE? *Please put your mind on hold while I look into my crystal ball and check my tea leaves.*
Permit me to suggest that past, present, and future exist in the *infinite present*. With that said, I can state without fear of contradiction that the *Infinite present* guarantees either of three certainties:

First, a not too distant time when *Greens* and women form *Green Earth Matriarchs,* a global movement that sweeps away greed, violence, and war. It will be a time of equality, plenty, and progress for everyone.

Mother Earth will be protected. Respect for and preservation of all life will be the highest priority. Stewardship of the Earth will be a major pursuit.

Social innovations in health, science, and technology will permit humanity to abundantly fulfill Earth-friendly energy needs, forging a path to the stars and into the Cosmos. The new society of equal rights, education, and opportunity will bring about a long overdue global reality of: '*Life, Liberty, and the pursuit of Happiness.*'

The *Second* option is the exact and disastrous opposite of the *First*. No more need be said about option two.

Option *Three,* as you might expect, is a combination of the two. The probability of option *Three* is the highest.

Contradictions: A progressive and peaceful *infinite present* requires the resolution of troubling contradictions:

1) More *Have profit* depends on less *Have-not income*;
2) Low *income* endangers the *family*;
3) Reduced *income* reduces buying and *consumption*;
4) Unpaid *housework* is dehumanizing;
5) *Private profit* denies *public needs*;
6) Housework begets *people*, wagework begets *profit*;
7) *Haves* consume the Earth; *Have-nots* eat crumbs;
8) *Have-nots* create *Have-wealth & Have-not poverty*;
9) Growing *Have* wealth for 0.2%, shrinks income for 99.8% of *Have-nots*;
10) *Distribution* and *sharing* is the problem, not profit;
11) *Socialized production* increases *privatized profit*;
12) Earth is victimized by *Have sociopaths*;
13) *Have Takers* believe: 'The Earth belongs to us, without limit. Defeat our competitors—destroy them and their access to everything; it's our God-given right to take it all.'

14) *Have-not Leavers* are Earth-friendly, tribal and communal people who take what they need and leave the rest.

Wanting can make it happen: is a fictional scenario that may already be in progress—(*MOM SAVES THE UNIVERSE,* Cosmic Energy, Global Peace, Reaching the Stars, a Feminist Future Reality Novel, http://www.amazon.com/Mom-Saves-the-Universe-Feminist-ebook/dp/B00MJKVYCM)

The Co-op created a global network of websites linking like-minded people. The *global energy co-op* continues to grow. It's a new world of communication freedom, with the potential of connecting billions of people. Of course, there's always a price to pay for freedom.

Unless there's money to be made, technology does not advance. As they say: ***Follow the money!***

Network lunacy is great fun; but the challenge is *mega-volt wireless* energy transmission with Tesla's high-power wireless technology, tech. Can graphene be used? Adapting programming code to *graphene* is promising. The strength and electrical properties of *graphene* are excellent. *Graphene* transistors can pack terabits of code.

Graphene can replace metal, silicon, and wireless tech. *Graphene* size is one-billionth of a meter, a nano-meter. It can be woven into fabric and even sprayed onto buildings.

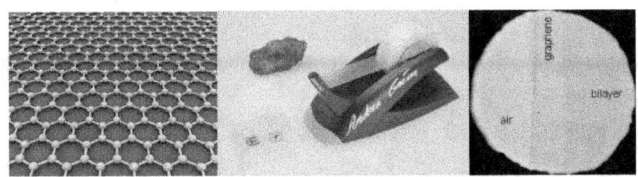

96-Graphene atomic-scale honeycomb lattice of carbon atoms;
97-Graphite lump, graphene transistor & tape dispenser;
98-Graphene one-atom-thick crystal naked eye light-photo;
http://en.wikipedia.org/wiki/Graphene

Graphene provides solar energy storage-retrieval and for **SuperCapacitors**, SCs, capable of reducing fuel costs up to 60%. http://en.wikipedia.org/wiki/Graphene

SCs are efficient devices for re-capturing lost energy when applying *breaks* on trains, buses, cars, and other transport. http://en.wikipedia.org/wiki/Supercapacitor

SCs save energy, reduce carbon dioxide emissions, and lower transportation costs.

The Co-op became energy self-sufficient; able to resell over half Co-op generated energy back to the power grid. Solar arrays and tree-top wind turbines fed power to five Co-op crafted generators on adjacent family sites. With flags and banners waving in the wind, flag-pole *piezo-wind-solar energy* was brought on-line.

A series of colorful flag-pole banners were arrayed with *piezo-electric* fibers woven into the fabric together with

143

thin-film solar nano-fibers. The small flexible quartz-like piezo fibers convert wind pressure directly to electricity.
http://en.wikipedia.org/wiki/Piezoelectricity

Co-opers build *parabolic solar dishes* for steam to power small electric graphene generators. Out-buildings house hand-made graphene generators. Greenhouse labs research and utilize *artificial leaf-tree photosynthesis*.
http://en.wikipedia.org/wiki/Renewable_energy#Artificial_photosynthesis

Greenhouse research extracts carbon dioxide, CO_2, from night plant respiration for synthesizing *graphene*. Baking soda and caustic soda are used in exhaust CO_2 filter traps.

Copper and metal parts are replaced with *graphene*. Mass production will eventually reduce graphene cost below copper. Co-opers now produce their own graphene for wiring, transistors, and other electronics.

Wiring generators with *graphene*, rather than copper, provides a ten-fold power increase. Graphene reduces metal weight.

Co-op people with electronic know-how built the first generator as a test model. Once the first was up and running, additional *graphene* generators were easier and faster to produce. The Co-op began planning commercial production of their *light-weight graphene generators, GenLites*. These were powered by *Bat-acitor* solar-wind batteries, modeled on SuperCapacitors.

144

Metal tools were replaced with Co-op machined *graphene* tools. *Graphene* replacement parts and tools were later die-cast from ceramic molds. *Graphene lock-staples* replaced welding. *GenLite graphene* generators were easily disassembled for relocation. Co-opers built a table-top solar-wind powered *GenLite* less than one cubic foot and only 25 pounds, easily powering a mid-size home.

Nola said, 'We have a fascinating tiger by the tail. I suggest we hang-on and plan this carefully. We need to put together a detailed proposal and outline a plan-of-action. Then we can discuss it with the entire Co-op.

'The idea of *Kudzu-Arthrospira-Naturals*, KANs can work. *Arthrospira* is the most common form of blue-green algae, *Cyanobacteria* or *Cyano.* http://en.wikipedia.org/wiki/Arthrospira

'The *Arthrospira* form of *Cyano* is widely used in food production as Spirulina. What do y'all think of that phrase: Yes we *KAN*? *Cyano* provides a boost to global health and Co-op cash flow.' http://en.wikipedia.org/wiki/Cyanobacteria

Kudzu is in the pea family. It's a nutritious food containing 50% protein and like *Cyano* contains a full complement of amino acids, vitamins, and minerals. *Kudzu* and *Cyano* are found in Asian markets as starch and gel for soups and sauces. 'We might consider this our pay-back to Mother Nature, as well as a promising commercial enterprise.

145

99-Cyanobacteria, Cyano, *blue-green algae Tolypothrix*;
100-Cyano *Nostoc pruniforme* colonies,
Cyano species are unicellular, colonial, filaments, sheets, or hollow balls;
101-Cyano Spirulina nutritional tablets

We have a full plate now. Notice the flexibility of *KAN*.'

102-103 Kudzu pea pods, on trees, and Japanese starch cake
http://en.wikipedia.org/wiki/Kudzu

Lela invited those interested to take part in the project. Part of the KAN plan is research and commitment from Co-opers. She asked Paul for his economic view.

Paul responded, 'My research examines the role of family in the global economy. Put simply: household income allows people to shop; that's a no-brainer. As income rises people are able to buy more stuff—big surprise.

146

'As income falls, there's less to spend, buying declines, and the economy spirals down into the global *Great Recession*. This is the 21st Century reality. Any innovation increasing cash-flow and benefits the Earth works for me.'

Back at the Co-op, family creation and energy pursuits were moving right along. In addition to a lovely crop of kids, there were: blue-green algae enhanced *raised-bed* sweet onions, peanuts, sweet potatoes, and soybeans.

Spraying a mixture of cat urine pheromone, cayenne pepper, and baking soda discouraged predators. Sweet onions, genetically modified with blue-green algae, were larger, greener, and sweeter than regular sweet onions.

The onion taste was distinct, but far sweeter than normal; tasting more like caramelized onion. There was not a tear in a bushel. *Cyano* sweet onion tasted like a *caramelized* dessert, but with the texture and crispness of onions.

It was the best tasting onion ever. Co-opers agreed it was the *ideal* onion.

Laura did most of the *sweet onion* research and suggested calling it: 'Blue-Green *Idealia* onion. Maybe just *Idealia-BG* will work. I think we should avoid commercial use of the word *Cyano,* as it suggests cyanide. We might promote our brand as: '*Idealia, the most delicious veggies you've ever tasted*; *they're ideal.*'

'*Idealia* is the first complete protein veggie, with all the necessary amino acids. For the health-conscious, *Idealia* surpasses meat in nutrient value. *Idealia* might be the Co-op trademark for all *Cyano* produce. It will encourage veggie diets. How about a gold halo in the *Idealia* logo?'

Kit added, 'We'll need to patent *Idealia-BG*. The *Idealia* technology will be copied—count on it. Can we get *Food and Drug* to recognize *Idealia-BG* crops as traditional foods, Generally Recognized as Safe, GRaS?

'So what does this lead to? It could lead to establishing a large-scale Cyano-Kudzu industry. It's not just a food—*Idealia* are ideal foods. FDA is likely to treat Idealia-BG as genetically modified corn. If we just make a mixture of Kudzu and Cyano, as a food additive like salt or sugar we could bypass the FDA, as both are well established foods.

'One surprise is that the sugar content of Cyano-wine is less than half of commercial wine.

Cyano-wine is *dry*, as most sugar is converted to alcohol. The advantage here is the prospect of carving-out a specialty market for carbonated *Idealia-Bubbly-Brut*.

'Over a 20-year period, no mutations or adverse side-effects were detected with *Idealia* foods. Most Co-op people add *Idealia* food to their diets, with remarkable results. People grow taller, leaner, and mentally sharper.

'Libido, sexual activity, intellect, and overall health are measurably enhanced in Co-opers. Most of the adults eating *Idealia* foods for a year or more added one to two inches to their height, even those over 50.'

Pal's blood tests found increased *growth hormone* in the taller Co-op people, as well as increased levels of *sex hormones*. Growth and sex hormone increase also results from increased fish consumption; that complicate testing.

Pal explained the role of sex hormones, 'Sexuality validates our existence, and provides strong social links. Sex stimulates imagination, intellect, and ultimately human progress. Of all human activities, sex most fully unites the human race thru family formation. This is why I agree that sexual activity affirms our physical and mental reality. Sex is more than a physical and intellectual benefit. On a spiritual level sex is a uniquely human affirmation. We are reborn every time we make love; at least that's my belief.

'Pornographers are those who use the media to sell violence, war; coercion, hoarding, and the abuse of unshared wealth. Violence and greed are economic porn.

'Media violence amounts to pornography, since sellers profiting from armaments, violence, and war prostitute humanity. War pornographers sell death and destruction.

'The rich and greedy consider they are the final product of evolution, the pinnacle of creation. They are the *Takers*. Arms dealers and peddlers of violence believe that myth. They justify all their actions as the right of superior beings. It's simply Nazi mentality.'

Jup took it upon himself to sum-up. 'Cyano began terra-forming billions of years ago; and continue the process into the 21st Century. They feed their increasing numbers on the added carbon dioxide people supply. Perhaps Cyano and plants need people to provide increasing amounts of carbon dioxide—do ya'll think?

'Notice the irony? Cyano create us and we *thinking* critters create Cyano by providing more carbon dioxide. Maybe Mother-Nature coded our DNA for this purpose. If humans are gone, plants would inherit the Earth. Would the Earth be better off without people? Plants and Cyano might think so, if they can think.'

Lela provided a question, in answer to Jup's question. 'Are you suggesting that global greed spear-heads the coming disaster of carbon dioxide over-load? I'll ask and answer my own question. It seems as if super-rich sociopaths follow each other over the environmental cliff—dragging the rest of humanity with them.'

Jup said, 'That's an interesting twist on the old idea of *determinism*. It's ludicrous to suggest Mother-Nature follows some coded plan. Is this some weird resurrection of *creation theory*?'

Lela answered, 'I merely suggest a cause and effect. Global greed pursues wealth without regard to out-come. The super-rich buy politicians and governments in the pursuit of profit. Maybe genetic code programs people—perhaps it's Mother-Nature's *invisible hand*?

'Don't you think it interesting? Social critters like ants and bees with social genetic code benefit their society as a whole. At the opposite end of genetic coding, we humans have individual conscious awareness, but seem deficient in social consciousness.

'Sex, love, family, and social cohesion are the primary human activities benefiting, rather than violating humanity. Yet the super-rich deny the power of sexuality, especially explicit sex. Patriarchs know sexuality is the power of matriarchs. Women's power is their sexuality. Down-play sex and women are kept-down.

'We have a lot of irons in the fire. Creating a viable industry with kudzu is challenge enough. *Idealia* as a health enhancer, life-extender, and growth promoter merely scratches the surface. *Cyano* and *Kudzu* together are ideal.

'Does this sound like a contradiction? We try to build a world thru safe-sane energy production. We see ourselves as angels of a better Earth, pitted against the destruction of

151

super-wealth. That's our myth. Perhaps carbon dioxide polluters serve *Cyano*, as well as Mother-Nature?'

Laura broke in, 'Why argue about this? We're better off working on how we can make things better. There's a real possibility *Idealia* could serve as catalytic media for producing meats without slaughtering livestock. Think of it, a world without animal slaughter: *Cultured meat* is cruelty-free meat, and is an animal-flesh product that has not resulted in a slaughtered critter, or genetic modification.

'We will of course face the issue of economic transition. As *cultured-meat* slowly replaces animal-slaughter, meat producers and workers are likely to pioneer *cultured-meat.* This is especially true as *cultured-meat* enterprises will reserves jobs for ex-meat workers. We'll make it a must.

'Just as wine, bread, and dairy yeast cultures are available, so too *meat cultures* could be available along with trained techies. Globalizing, localizing, and decentralizing food production could change humanity for the better. This can be compared to moonshine brewing, as an actual model. Home *meat-culture* may be feasible.

'We're building a progressive Co-op. We're family, friends, lovers, researchers, and explorers searching for energy. That's our myth. It's the story we tell ourselves.'

'What will happen if we expand too rapidly? Will it explode like a balloon, or just exhaust us? I'm suggesting we slow down, think about it all, and discuss it realistically. We're living in an age when energy information is freely available. Many successful cooperatives devolved into commercial success. Oneida is one that comes to mind:

Oneida was an 1848 religious commune. They believed that Jesus returned in AD 70, allowing Oneida to bring about *Jesus's millennial kingdom*, and be free of sin and perfect in this world and Heaven. Oneida practiced *Communalism*; that is communal sharing of property and possessions.

Oneida strongly believed that any member was free to have sex with any other consenting member. Possessiveness and exclusive relationships were discouraged. They believed the natural outcome of sex was pregnancy; and raising children should be a communal responsibility. Women over 40 were to act as sexual *mentors* to adolescent boys and religious role models for young men. Older men introduced young women to sex.
http://en.wikipedia.org/wiki/Oneida_Community

'Oneida is interesting as a commune that took the commercial route, but it's not a model for us. I suggest we slow down; list the options; discuss the pros and cons; do

153

the research as needed; and debate each proposal fully before acting on any major project.

'In this regard, consider that biological processes form a *Bell-Curve* of start-peak-end. For us it's birth-life-death. We can't change the sequence, but we can skew it. We can extend the curve by fine-tuning the central peak. This means we should slow down and take stock of what we really want. Those of us deciding on a progressive, socially responsible life can continue to create within our Co-op.

'Those commercially inclined can satisfy their personal enterprise urge outside the Co-op, while still remaining an active part of Co-op activities. Can't we have both a progressive Co-op and commercial success?'

Lela added, 'If we commercialize our Co-op, I believe it will destroy our purpose. Modest local success is not the problem, but large-scale commercialization would ruin the Co-op. Outside profiteers would gain control. Let's think about this over the next week and talk again.' Most Co-opers agreed and gave Lela appreciative hugs.

Laura had the final word: 'Between discussions and *Wiki* we have access to a wealth of information. I suggest we track energy research, discuss the more promising ideas, and think about what can work for our Co-op, before going down blind alleys.'

An old Unitarian hymn has the phrase: *Our Bones Link Stones to Stars*; suggesting our cosmic links. As the world economy crumbles, some have their eyes on the stars. They pursue *energy* in the belief that a wealth of shared energy can become the great leveler.

They reason: If there was enough cheap *energy*, global problems would fade away. Since all stuff comes from the stars, so too does all *energy*. If the Cosmos and Earth are bundles of *energy*, then the pursuit of *energy* is the most promising endeavor.

Kit began the writers meeting: 'The *Energy Compendium* will be an on-going global network freely available in summary and in detail to subscribers.

'The first of the *Energy Compendium* entries is **Cold Fusion**: *Cold fusion* is a room temperature nuclear reaction, while *hot fusion* requires extreme heat. Researchers continue to investigate *cold fusion*; now called ***low-energy nuclear reactions***.

'*Cold fusion* is included in the *Energy Compendium* exactly because it's a long-shot, providing a record of the pit-falls awaiting energy researchers. It provides a continuing drama and helps to anchor our hopes in reality.

'We will attempt to identify factors contributing to successful *Cold fusion* experiments and record these. The

155

most recent *energy* initiative concerns research into subatomic particles as potential energy break-throughs.

'Before dismissing *Hot-fusion*, consider the latest breakthrough: Engineers designed a small *Hot-fusion* reactor. When scaled up to a large electrical power plant, it rivals a new coal-fired plant in terms of cost and output.'

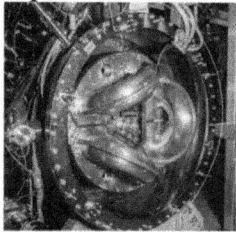

104-HIT-SI3 hot fusion engine is one-tenth size of the
Power-producing Dynomak, University of Washington
http://www.sciencedaily.com/releases/2014/10/141008131156.htm

'The idea that basic energy particles such as light *photons* can give birth to photon twins captures the imagination. These speculative energy studies are published on popular scientific web-sites and in journals.

An ***entanglement-wormhole*** is a case in point. *Instantaneous action at a distance* occurs much faster than the speed of light. Einstein's *spooky action at a distance* can only be understood as a *wormhole* between two distant photon twins. Instant communication between all cosmic points is equivalent to light-speed cubed or 35 quintillion

156

miles per second, linking all cosmic points in a fraction of a second. Is that instant enough for you?'

West Texas Petroplex shale-oil potential in the 1970's was considered the largest petroleum reserve in the world. In 2014, new horizontal drilling technology began producing a flood of oil. http://www.energyandcapital.com/articles/west-Texas-oil/4108

In 2015 the U.S. not only became oil self-sufficient, but also the world's largest and cheapest oil source. Proven reserves of at least 36 billion barrels were verified in just two leases.

The major initial problem was inadequate oil pipeline and distribution. The transport-export system was ill-equipped to handle the flood of oil. This resulted in backed-up rail oil tankers, and slowed grain shipments.

By the time the infra-structure was fully upgraded in 2020, cheaper renewable energy undercut petrol demand. Green energy research and production is now the leading global pursuit.

Green energy and climate remediation initiated new industries. Huge coastal-ocean algae farms produce renewable petroleum, food, and the reduction of atmospheric carbon dioxide. Ocean petroleum shipping declines, as algal coastal farming spreads globally.

Meg, a geo-physicist from Cork, Ireland moved into the Co-op. Nola recruited Meg based on her work with the

157

Irish Energy Board. It started as an oil-drilling and gas fracking venture; but Meg helped change that.

Based on her achievements in *Earth-magnetics*, Meg was recruited to establish the Tesla Center for Energy Research. She chaired the Irish Energy Board as a result of her breakthrough, accomplishing what was thought impossible. Meg's team built *Earth-magnetic energy* into an industry.

Meg led a team in a ten-year effort that is marginalizing fossil fuels. The need for petroleum declines as fast as *Earth-magnetic energy* replaces it.

Meg's team developed two innovations supporting **Earth-Magnetic-Energy, EMag**. The first is the **super-conductor, SuDuc;** and the other is the **EMag Bat-acitor** for energy storage.

Particle Accelerator research initiated these efforts; but covert interest in *particle-beam* weapons account for much of the funding. Graphene development helped make **EMag** a reality.

Ireland is now the global center for geo-magnetic energy and the world's first energy commonwealth. *EMag* is held in common-trust for the Irish people, at home and in the diaspora that is now reversing. As the Irish Energy Board financed Meg's research team, all patents, licensing, and industry applications belong to the Irish Commonwealth. There are no losers in the energy game. Investors in fossil

158

energy are invited to transfer investments to Ireland's new global *EMag* holdings.

While the Irish Commonwealth holds firm control, the nations of the world and the fossil fuel establishment are encouraged to partake in the new global energy banquet. *'Energy wealth for all'* became the global motto.

The Matron Steward of Ireland declared, 'There's a place for all of us at Energy-Mother's banquet.' Share-holders are persuaded, not just by the model of the Irish Commonwealth, but also by investment terms.

International Energy Law now requires all energy wealth be shared with *EMag* workers, consumers, and investors. Just as national investment in geo-magnetic energy is financed from *public revenue*, the dividends are held in trust for all families.

Some ask, 'Where do the *public revenue* come from?' The answer is: All financial transactions by Irish citizens are subject to a stiff *surcharge*. Irish energy investment is insured and functions like an annuity, with a ten-year 10% average annual return.

Irish citizens are free to invest in anything, anywhere in the world, but investment transactions are subject to the same *surcharge*, based on citizenship.

Investing outside your nation, you pay your money and take your chances. There's no guaranteed return on investment. Most nations are adapting similar financial arrangements.

Beginning in Ireland, the *family* was for the first time officially recognized as the *factory* producing people. All Irish families are now designated *EMag* investors. *EMag* dividends are shared by all families.

The reverse diaspora and increasing birth rate provide Ireland with a population of ten-million. The inspiration for Ireland was Alaska families sharing petroleum wealth.

Ireland is the first *new-energy* nation to educate her people to '*Give your best to get the best.*' The Irish Commonwealth is on its way to become the first matriarchy.

Matriarch stewardship arrives on the heels of increasing *EMag* wealth. Dublin, Waterford, and Cork are fast becoming a single metro area as they grow together along the southeast 'Gold Coast.'

Hydraulic fracturing was known since the 1970s. Magnetic energy is stronger at deeper depth. Old gas and oil well shafts provide *EMag* access. This strategy provides great savings.

Super-conductor cable is installed and well-heads are capped with *Bat-acitors* for energy storage and transfer. It's similar to the way fiber-optic cable is run thru old natural gas pipes. Tesla-wave wireless transmitters transfer

EMag along the old power lines. Power lines are removed as a wireless **Bat-acitor** replaces a power line junction.

In spite of deep drilling *faults*, the *features* were soon realized. Not only can natural gas replace petrol, but *EMag* can eventually replace all fossil fuel.

With research in vat-controlled algae production, the world realizes that algae are the primary petroleum source. Since algae can be produced in ocean farms as well as in sewage-treatment ponds, micro-algae are competitive with solar bio-reactors. While a market for algae fuel oil will continue, *EMag* will eventually replace most, if not all carbon-based fuels.

We are at the point of ending fracking and petrol drilling. *EMag* energy production uses fossil fuel infrastructure, but without further environmental damage. This is where our Tech team and Tesla research group interact with the Irish Energy Board.

No one says *EMag* will be too cheap to meter; but *EMag* supply over the last five years was more efficient, plentiful, Earth-friendly, and far less costly than fossil fuel. Most important, *EMag* is as safe and plentiful as wind and solar.

'Before ending this video, I feel the need to state a personal belief: people would benefit if patriarchal sex prejudice were relegated to the dust-bin of history. For the last 2,500 years it has largely been *his-story*.

'His attitude toward sex is one of paranoid possession—*owning* women and children by controlling sex is the patriarchal reality behind sex morality. This extends to *patriarchal possession* and *property*.

'Patriarchy subverts love and sex with the primacy of violence, war, profit, and greed. The same can be said about our deep-seated attitudes concerning human equality—specifically the right to live and share the resources provided by Mother-Nature. I pledge to work for human equality and the wellbeing of all Mother-Nature's children. I'm adding this it to the video.'

'Fat storage relates to nitrogen-protein deprivation in algae. Algae store oil when deprived of nitrogen. Poor health may result from high carb-fat intake together with a low protein diet. Are algae sending us a message?'

Nola answered, 'It makes sense. Why didn't we think of it? We've a full plate and some ideas are bound to fall thru the cracks. Pal, I think you hit on an important link—lack of protein-nitrogen is linked to excess fat and oil build-up.

'High protein kudzu flour is now part of most processed foods. Virtually every market sells cake mixes, flour, bread, and baked goods with the promotional label, *Kudzu enriched*.

'We see kosher food with a 'K' symbol. Now it's common to see '*Kz*' indicating kudzu. Often the first

162

ingredient listed on product labels is kudzu—usually 10% or more since it's a cheap food.

'The World Health Organization reports a decline in population growth where high protein kudzu and Cyano foods are widely used. I talked with Pal about this as he has a background in animal nutrition.

'Pal mentioned research suggesting a relationship between protein consumption and human fertility. As more protein was consumed, infant mortality declined, as did human fertility, and birthrates. Healthy kids seem to reduce the need and desire for having more children. Kudzu-blue-green algae *KUDGEE* foods were available since antiquity, but were largely limited to Asian diets.'

The first *Energy Compendium* entry is **Fusion Hot and Cold.** The most recent *energy* initiative concerns research in subatomic particles as potential energy break-throughs. The idea that light *photons* can *birth* photon twins continues to capture the imagination.

Long-shot energy studies are published on scientific web-sites. **Entanglement-wormhole** is a case in point. *Instantaneous action at a distance* occurs much faster than light-speed. Einstein's *spooky action at a distance* can be understood as a *worm-hole* between distant photon twins.

Regarding quantum probability, Einstein said, 'God does not play dice;' but *cosmic Mother* deals with probabilities, even if Father God does not.

'Science fiction writers say, 'If you can imagine it, then it will happen.' That's why I'd like to add to the *Speculative energy* web page: *Zero-point energy, Cosmic Microwave Background Radiation, Dark energy, Monopole energy,* and *Black hole energy.* Imagine it and it happens! Nothing is so *far-out* that we can't at least list it in the *Speculative Energy* section.'

We now realize subatomic energy particles, such as photons and electrons, provide the foundation of *mental* and *physical reality*—perhaps a *spiritual* reality as well.

The fact that a quadrillion body cells have their own means of *chemical, electromagnetic,* and *photon* communication suggests all stuff is *energy*: connected, intelligent, replicating, recycling, and alive. If *reality* is *energy* then cosmic reality is independent of human senses.

The same geometric code appears in living cells and the Cosmos. The same **spiral curve** is found in galaxies, ear whorls, finger prints, nautilus shells, and in DNA. It's the code of *energy* and physical reality.

There's a new voyage of discovery. Research in nano-tech *graphene,* biotech-genetics, and *Entanglement*

105-Tattooed Fertility Votive Hacilar, Turkey 5,000 BC

provide a unique view of *energy*. ***Feed-back loops*** of all stuff comprise the code of *energy*. All these actions require *code*. *Consciousness* may now be defined as the sum of brain *feed-back loop code*.

Perhaps subatomic particles lack conscious awareness, but they have *intelligence* in the form of *geometric code*. *Genetic code* provides all the *intelligence* needed. A large *quantity* of interactive brain neuron feed-back loops provides a change in brain neuron *quality*—it's a qualitative shift in ***consciousness***. This is part of energy *reality*.

'We exist as subatomic-, atomic-, molecular-, cellular-, and genetic-*code*. It's a lot of *code*. It's a huge amount of *intelligence*. Does all stuff ***know*** without *consciousness?*

Perhaps they ***know*** in the Biblical sense of intimate links. Just as we have knowledge of each other on many levels, sexual intimacy provides a level of ***knowing*** that does not require conscious awareness.

It's suggested that the origin of sexual energy is magnetic negative and positive electrical charge.

Cyano, our ancestral mothers, have a high level of code intelligence; but they don't *know* they convert water and carbon dioxide to energy in the presence of sunlight. Do *Cyano know* the waste oxygen they give off supports respiration for other critters? Cyano act as if they *know*; but they follow a *code*, a built-in genetic *program*.

It's suspected that **conscious awareness** is a less important part of **intelligence** than we care to admit. *Consciousness* may be as much a *fault* as a *feature*. Our quadrillion body cells function quite well without *conscious awareness*.

106-Eye Goddess Brak, in three forms, Denmark 20,000 BC

From an *Information Age* we enter the ***Age of Intelligence***. We enter an era of *networking, programming, coding,* and *intelligence*. Is it going to be an *information* age or the *age of intelligence*? There's already too much *information*. What's needed is the *intelligence* to deal with it.

166

The real frontier is genetic coding. Humanity is on the brink of an energy revolution and I suggest it begins with *coding*.

Drone pilot *thoughts* program aircraft to fly. *Thought-pilots* learn to clench their right fist to achieve a right turn. An up-turned fist moves the drone aircraft upward. This is a hint of the possibilities that an *Age of Intelligence* may bring. Mind Over Matter, MOM, is now a reality. http://www.popularmechanics.com/science/health/nueroscience/piloting-a-quadcopter-with-the-power-of-thought-15556867

Meg added, 'Magnetic energy is extracted like oil. Tesla believed geo-magnetic *fields* could be *cut* like fields of wheat and magnetic energy pumped like oil. There are electromagnetic *aurora borealis*, solar wind, and *magnetars* throughout the cosmos. Magnetar SGR 1900+14 is in the exact center of the infrared image below; its gas ring is seven light years across.' (Spitzer Space Telescope)

107-Magnetar is visible only in X-ray light.
http://en.wikipedia.org/wiki/Magnetar

Magnetic energy is as ubiquitous throughout the Cosmos as solar energy. *Electromagnetism* is necessary for life.

167

Molten iron forms a circulating electro-magnetic liquid, functioning like an Earth-size dynamo. Think of all the magnetic energy in the Earth-dynamo. *EMag* taps into it.

108-Indus Valley Fertility Goddess 2,000 BC

Magnetic energy taps into all life. We see this when non-magnetic cloth and paper are charged with static-electricity—static-cling, the demon of the fashion world. The point I'm clumsily making is that magnetic energy is the basis of all life and energy, or so I believe.

We have our own more intimate electro-magnetic *dynamo,* with the heart as the pumping station. Animals, plants, and minerals depend on *magnetic energy transfer*. Perhaps the real ***life-force*** is ***electromagnetism***.

17-YEAR 2090: *This is the story of my mom. It's also the story of how Matriarchs ended global violence using global energy. Mom is now global First Matriarch and we couldn't be more proud.*
The Earth-Family now includes communities in the Moon, Europa, and Mars, as well as planetary exploration

families. The Matriarch Space Agency now trains entire families for exploratory and colonizing missions. Usually two to six families go on joint missions.

The ten years from 2025 to 2035 is officially the *Transition Time*. As far as I'm concerned it was a time of world-wide disasters, and die-offs. At least 4-billion people died. That's just a rough estimate. No one knows the actual number. It's taken 55 years to move on. Mom says 'progress is the only way to honor our dead.'

It was the idiot men, our bogus leaders. Using a strong magnetic field, an attempt was made to *protect* Earth from *aliens* by reforming the Asteroid Belt into an Earth-Shield.

The result was catastrophic, to say the least. They called it Project Sky Shield; as if aliens would be deterred by an Asteroid shield. The idea of protective fortresses died along with male leadership.

Alien *visitors* are here and everywhere; they assure us we are all aliens. We think about a question and the *visitors* the answer instantly in our head. They say everything in the Cosmos is alien and yet a part of the same cosmic family.

If the cosmic *visitors* are nothing else, they are certainly philosophers. The *visitors* insist they are describing the true cosmic reality; it's not philosophy. We think philosophy is speculative thought. *Visitors* say they do not speculate.

The ancients referred to the Asteroid Belt as the *Heavenly Necklace*. Our spaced-out leaders broke the Necklace and the pieces rained down on Earth for almost ten years.

The smallest, most unstable asteroids were dislodged. As with lightening, most struck oceans or burnt up entering Earth's atmosphere. We were lucky; it could have been worse, or so our leaders said at the time. What else could they say? The *visitors* say they tried to warn our departed leaders; but they would not take the *visitors* seriously.

Our *star-sisters* saved us from the worst of it; but even the *all-knowing* can't work miracles. I don't know why we call them *star-sisters*. The only sex they have is akin to positive and negative magnetic poles, or so they say.

They don't actually say anything. We ask questions and know the answers before finishing the question. The *visitors* say it's a type of radio transmission.

Mom asked about their physical nature. Instantly she realized they are diffuse energy clouds. Asking where they come from, she knew they are everywhere, always. I asked why I don't understand. Immediately I got the gentle answer: 'When you are ready to know, you will.'

As it stands, we lost over half the human population and the decimation of many plants and animals. The asteroids that made land-fall were bad enough; but the ocean-falls caused ten years of tsunamis inundating global coast-lines.

109-Kokle Hopi Earth Mother 1,000 BC

The sadness and dread expressed by *Kokle Hopi*, above, reflects the feelings survivors live with. Since most people and cities bordered coastal areas, these suffered most.

Highlands 1,000 feet above sea level were spared; but coastlines were decimated. It's not known how Australia and New Zealand were spared, but we're thankful nevertheless. Larger asteroids dislodged the partially melted polar ice-caps. Polar melts added to sea-levels.

They say die-offs occur every 10 to 15 thousand years, with or without help from people; guess we were over-due. It took two years to convince *coastals* to move to higher ground. Most of the die-off was in the first two years.

Entire nations were washed away. Those taking refuge in the mountains and highlands survived. It's estimated there were three-billion survivors.

Global male leadership was washed away or buried, as was their military and policing apparatus. Asteroid impact, polar melt, and sea rise resulted in an incalculable number of earth-quakes and plate-tectonic shifts.

Magnetic pole shift continues, but slowly. Virtually all leaders in deep shelter-cities were buried with their families. Mountain ranges rose, fell, and rose again. Underground shelters became burial tombs. Archeologists will have a great career when they excavate a mile or two into the Earth.

The handful of escapees suffered post-traumatic-stress, severe survivor guilt, as well as mental instability. Global male leadership was at an end. Cynics suggest Mother-Nature did the world a favor; but most of us are saddened by the loss. After all, we are all mothers' children.

United Earth Matriarchs are shifting the New Worlds Resettlement program into over-drive. More than 100 matriarch republics now coordinate space programs.

110-Hopi Spider Mother Sun handle plate, 1000 BC

The Hopi visuals suggest prophesies similar to what we experienced. Hopi legend mentions the starving Earth Mother consumes her children. That sounds about right.

The Good News: The Matriarch Republic of Atlanta-Montreal, MRAM, is now one of the most important global

Republics. It stretches thru Appalachia all the way to the Laurentians in Montreal, Quebec. We are the lucky ones. Including refugees, population is now over100 million.

The MRAM includes: Blue Ridge, Ozark, Appalachia, Shenandoah, and Adirondack MR Localities. The United States is history; it was literally *his-story*. Both the 'men' and the 'nation' remain sad memories.

Hundreds of global Matriarch Republics throughout the world are in close contact; forming a global federation. The Eurasian MR ranges from Siberia, Mongolia and Tibet, through the Himalayas, to the Ural-Aral region, and is contiguous thru the Middle East to Turkey. Their census two years ago claimed a population of one billion. It is by far the largest MR.

Pacifica MR from Mexico to Alaska claims 300 million. Andes MR with 300 million stretches from ice-free Antarctica to the rising Caribbean Islands. Alp-Pyrenees MR claims 400 million.

While most global land is under water, other areas have become *high-rise* real estate. Most significant is the Anzak MR, now contiguous with a warming Antarctica, Tasmania, Australia, New Zealand, New Guinea, and the Solomon Islands, with 100 million people.

The Atlantic-Scandia MR stretches from a greening Greenland to Iceland, Ireland, England, and Scotland thru

Scandinavia. These are still rising, more than a thousand feet so far. It forms a land bridge with 100 million people.

The south of Ireland is becoming a tropical Riviera, rivaling Hawaii. A broad spectrum of palm trees and tropical plants is transforming Ireland into a global tropical conservatory. In addition to its booming *EMag* sector, Ireland is becoming a global tourist attraction.

The biggest surprise is the rise of the Hawaiian MR, now half the size of Australia, but with only 30 million people, mostly Asian immigrants.

The Earth is now a maritime federation with open global immigration, without visas or passports. In fact, most MRs welcome immigration.

Ireland's tourist board now offers gratis, transport on new luxury catamaran magnetic levitation ships, *CatLevs*. Other Matriarch Republics follow Ireland's lead. Magnetic levitation *FlyBys* serve air travel needs.

Progress is the result of matriarch stewardship. Matriarch Republics now forge ahead. Of the 200 MR nations, mom got 90% of the vote. Mom was chosen because she transformed the Atlanta-Montreal MR into a model of humane Earth-friendly scientific progress.

Mom provides a hopeful humane future by initiating the New Worlds Resettlement program, and gaining the cooperation of over 100 space-savvy nations.

Next month families in Moon, Mars, and other settlements will be permitted three-month rotation to and from Earth.

In celebration, we're helping mom with her global inaugural address, **Beginnings**. It's a *HoloVid* about our place in the infinite ocean of cosmic energy.

It's no great mystery now; but early in the 21st Century people were confused. We now know we are bundles of *space-time atoms* swimming in an infinite ocean of cosmic energy. In fact, everything in the Cosmos is swimming with us. All energy is the center of the infinite Cosmos, including us. How do we know? The *visitors* told us so.

Mom says the cosmic center is everywhere. Talk about being the center of attention! We are told that matriarchs advance because they stand on the shoulders of men. Great granddad said they talked that way 100 years ago: Men advance because they stand on the shoulders of women.

Well, turn-about is fair play. Let's face it; if it were not for the global disaster, would a global matriarchy be possible? Eventually maybe; but *eventually* is a long time.

What would the Earth be like if male leadership continued? I shudder to think. Everyone says the return of global matriarchy was inevitable. It would have happened sooner or later. *WikiLites* document the first 997,500 years of matriarchal humanity.

It's understandable that climate change, totalitarian farming, and the resulting population explosion set the scene for the last 2,500 years of patriarch *inhumanity*.

Now that ten years of disastrous asteroid storms decimated the global population, mothers of the world are once again called upon to salvage the global family, much as mothers have always done for their own families.

111-Triple Goddess Vall Torta Ravine, Spain 40,000 BC

Key parts of **Beginnings** follow: In the beginning there is no beginning, rather there are cycles and re-cycles. Imagine Cosmic Mother expanding her energy from a single ultra-dense energy point into the Cosmos we know and love.

We now know ***Dark stuff*** is *dark energy* and *dark matter*. The *visitors* say, '*Dark energy* is the glue, the scaffold, and foam unifying all energy, all parallel worlds, and all dimensions.

From *Dark stuff* emerge a cosmic ocean of ionized energy *plasma,* vibrating into *energy strings*. Like strings on a violin, different vibrations provide the energy for the *music of the cosmic spheres.*'

Vibrating *energy strings* produce photons, quarks, electrons, protons, neutrons, and all subatomic critters. *Dark stuff* fills every part of the Cosmos. It's the stuff in which electrons orbit atoms.

Dark stuff is the cosmic ocean in which our quadrillion body cells swim. All energy is recycled in *Dark stuff;* it's what we call *space.* It's the cosmic womb of birth, life, and transition. What else have the *visitors* confirmed?

We now know *dark-energy* and *zero-point* energy are linked by *Quantum matter.* http://en.wikipedia.org/wiki/Zero-point_energy Stephen Hawking suggested *black holes* are hot, linking: *gravity, space-time, quantum matter*, and *thermal* energy in *Black Hole Thermodynamics.* http://en.wikipedia.org/wiki/Black_hole

Fay Dowker suggested *black hole thermodynamics* point to *space-time atomic granularity* at Planck-scale energy levels. Thank you *visitors*! http://en.wikipedia.org/wiki/Fay_Dowker

This energy level is the smallest possible amount of energy short of zero. It's the origin of the term *zero-point energy.* We now create *causal-set* code to manipulate quantum gravity for use in null-gravity *FlyBys.* Our space program is based on Tesla's gravity-creating engine.

All energy is part of an infinitely expanding-contracting Cosmos, without beginning or end. Cosmic energy endlessly re-cycles, in various phases of transition. At the end of each cycle, Mother Cosmos expands, cools, and restarts a new energy cycle.

177

Perhaps *Dark stuff* is a form of electromagnetic energy. *Dark stuff* theory is incomplete, lacking adequate data. The *visitors* say 'You're on the right track; so continue the research on your own. You have a right to your own discovery.'

112-Egyptian Isis and Horus mother and child 3,000 BC

When sunlight *photons* strike our skin, electrons heat the skin. One quadrillion body cells and microbes produce light photons, heat, and exchange electromagnetic energy. The human body is a crowded place; but it all seems to work.

It all depends on curved motion, from electron orbits, to planetary elliptics, and spiral galaxies. *Curvature* accelerates cosmic energy; in fact it seems *curvature* IS the cosmic energy generator, or so the *visitors* have confirmed.

If a researcher lacks hard experimental data, she can always theorize. This is the case with the *Big Bang*. Does anyone know how hot it was at the time of the *Big Bang*, or when it happened, or even if it happened? Rather than a *Big-Bang,* it could as easily be a *Big Whimper.*

Visitors are our tutors. They say that instinct, theory, and speculation are messages sent by our DNA.

Imagine cycles of *life* where all forms of *energy* are *alive,* in *motion, replicating,* and *intelligent.* Of course intelligence-code is a matter of degree. To put it bluntly: *energy is everything and everything is energy.* Referring to the *fabric* of space-time, Einstein suggested that **gravity is curvature.** Is all **energy curvature**? Yes it is!

Mother Nature perpetually assembles, disassembles, transforms, and recycles *energy* into: code, intelligence, data, programs, information, and even people. Cosmic energy *maintenance* amounts to cosmic *housework.* Mothers understand this. It's an *energy web,* and includes all critters, living in a womb of *Dark stuff.*

We all belong and have our place on Earth and in the Cosmos, simply because we exist as bundles of energy. We exist in the Cosmos as Mother-Nature's children. In one form or another, in one cosmic cycle or another, *we are always here,* without beginning or end.

Death is merely an energy transition, since energy is neither created nor destroyed, but only transformed. Our *energy* is always some-place; and that's better than being no-place. It's great that *visitors* can confirm our theories.

179

113-Hathor-Isis Egyptian cow goddess 2,000 BC

Neanderthal humans appeared about one million years ago. *Modern Gyna/Homo sapiens* evolved in Africa about 200,000 years ago. They were *modern* in that skull, and bone DNA from that period were the same as today.

The term *Gyna/Homo sapiens* refers to the genetic, mental, and physical differences between the sexes. The primary difference may be the nerve connections in the brain.

Corpus collosum connections *between* the two hemispheres of the brain are usually more numerous in women. *Within* the hemispheres, men tend to have more connections. This distinction provides women, especially mothers, with the ability to see the *big family picture*.

Mothers are equipped with brain neurons allowing them to comprehend and keep track of all family members. They are the first to spot family problems and opportunities.

This is why mothers are biologically equipped as matriarchs. Mothers become Matriarchs to the extent they treat the human family as their own kin.

When asked, *visitors* agree that *'mother knows best.'*

We've seen *age reversal* since the break-thru in stem-cell neuron regeneration in 2015. It amounts to restoring cellular energy; resetting the cellular clock. The reversal of Alzheimer's was the first practical achievement.

Hundreds of *Quantum Entanglement* experiments provide the incredible conclusion that photons are instantly shared throughout the Cosmos. *Visitors* now tell us it's egotistical to ask about what we have already proven.

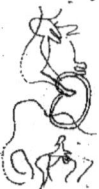

114-Fertility-Hunt goddess & mammoth
Pech-Merle Cave, France 50,000 BC

Now we have achieved *Entanglement* not only with masses of photons, but also with atoms, molecules, and even living cells. We know *Entanglement* is not merely a cosmic event, but occurs in all living cells.

As usual, our knowledge remains *incomplete*. We hope the knowledge quest is endless. Entanglement targets nano-bit stem-cell *drones*. Genetic modifications are achieved with the aid of computer guidance to specific gene switches and neurons.

181

The Cosmos is strange, but *energy* is even stranger. Photons transform into electrons; and while there is no death, we are not aware of our *energy* cycles. We are unaware of these transformations; but we can be certain our energy and all energy are always recycled.

18-ENERGY FUTURES: *Distinction between past, present, and future is only a stubbornly persistent illusion*—Albert Einstein.

The *MagCar* glides silently toward the patio. Like the old *Maglev* magnetic levitation trains, *MagCars* use magnetic levitation for power. Earth's magnetic field allows the *MagCar* to hover less than an inch above ground.

New energy ideas are rapidly adopted. Since energy is now the *currency*, this is to be expected. We exchange *Global Energy Units*, GEUs, as debits and credits.

Our needs and labors equate to electronic GEUs. Our research, income, consumption, education, health, entertainment, and even investments are instantly transferred to the local GEU *cloud*.

Mother-Nature's only guideline is: *Equal distribution of energy to all as needed; and from all as ability permits.* Money, banking, and the abuse of hoarded wealth are cast into the dust-bin of *His-story*. Matriarch humane innovation speeds energy and human progress; that's *Her-story*.

Earth-magnetics, *EMag*, and synthetic photosynthesis, *PhoSyn*, are the energy jewels in Mother-Nature's crown.

Also important are nano-tech, hot/cold fusion, and *Dyson Spheres*: Satellite Rings, Swarms, Bubbles, and Shells, for Solar Energy Retrieval:

115-Dyson Simple Ring
116-Dyson Swarm complex ring
117-Dyson Bubble solar stationary satellites
118-Dyson Shell, cut-away of Dyson's original concept
http://en.wikipedia.org/wiki/Dyson_sphere

Dyson Spheres are satellites around stars, such as our Sun. *Dysons* capture a portion of a stars' energy output. They were first described by Freeman Dyson as satellite-based structures for meeting escalating energy needs. Dyson proposed searching these to detect advanced intelligence.

Project *Solar-Moms* began by launching 360 small solar energy satellites in stationary orbit between the Sun and Mercury. Solar energy is relayed to and between *Bat-acitors, Bats,* via laser-pulse and then to Moon collectors.

Earth generators tap into *Moon-Bats* when Earth generators are energy deficient. It's safer and more efficient to use *Moon-Bats* for energy storage as *Bat* overload can occur.

Photosynthetic extraction of atmospheric CO_2 provides low-cost *graphene* synthesis and reduces atmosphere CO_2.

Property is now *globalized,* not *privatized.* Land use is now based on utility, not privilege. Property is leased from local Matriarch land-agents and traded back, but not owned.

119-Thrace Fertility Votive, bone and copper 3,000 BC

Population increased with the advent of the *Erotic-Media* re-population campaign of 2040. Admittedly, birth incentives got out of hand. The last global census confirmed almost five-billion. Most Matriarch Republics agreed five-billion is sufficient recovery.

Matriarchs aim for population stability. *Cultured meat* seems to do the job. Since the years of *cultured meat* success, population growth is limited to replacement.

Global improvement in nutrition, health, and economic security prompt people to have fewer children; providing incentives for taking better care of fewer kids. A key tool in population stability is replacing the *Erotic-Media* blitz with the *Global Progress thru Stability* blitz.

Electromagnetic Graphene is the key to health, longevity, and a multitude of energy applications.

184

As Alice said, *It's always jam yesterday, jam tomorrow, but never jam today.* Now we can truly be say, '*finally its jam today.*' http://en.wikipedia.org/wiki/Through_the_Looking-Glass

The global economic crash of 2025 is credited with the turn-around in energy and human prospects. The crash cleared the playing field. Matriarchs now replace Patriarchs. Human *need* now replaces *greed*.

We are in the midst of an energy revolution. Skilled techies are in short supply, but a living-wage is no longer an issue. Global population loss is replaced thanks to the Matriarch reproduction initiative.

Now population is stable. If we are to maintain the pace of progress, then training and education must be accelerated. Progress is credited to Matriarch stewardship and global partnering.

On land, sea, and in the air, *MagCars, CatLevs,* and *FlyBys* meet our transportation needs. *MindOverMatter, MOM,* was previously named *MindView* by the military. Now that we've directed our efforts toward peace and progress, MOM is a more accurate term for 'thought control.' MOM is now a media sensation along with *SkyView, BrainNet,* and *CellNet*. Based on the electroencephalograph, head-band like *EyeWraps* provides electromagnetic skin sensors.

185

EyeWraps provide skin-surface contacts with *BrainNet* brain neurons. Linking *CellNet, BrainNet,* and *MOM* permit real-time virtual access to Inner Planet Networks. We access life in over 100 Moon *cavern* communities. Tunneling mega-lasers liberate oxygen and water steam from vaporized rock. Tunneling proceeds at 300 feet daily.

Mars *terra-forming* families relay monthly progress. Hopefully, *Cyanobacteria* can do for Mars what *Cyano* did for Earth. The jury is still out on Project Cyano.

While hundreds of water-ice and dry-ice areas are mapped, no sign of microbial life, or any form of life has been found. Cyano will be *seeded* only in *wet* areas proven to be lifeless.

120-Nimrud, Iraq goddess head 800 BC

MindOverMatter, MOM, began as a weapon 100 years ago. This is the case with many technologies, such as duct-tape, Teflon, transistors, Internet, drones, and robot house-cleaning, *RoboClean*. The *MagCar* is a recent spin-off from defense research. *Mars-rover* solar powered robots were early steps in this direction. Now that all technology and resources are freely shared with all global matriarchies

186

there's no reason for covetous aggression. Military budgets shrink in cost from trillions to thousands. With the end of male leadership, global aggression rapidly evaporates.

EMag use in Tesla Wireless magnetic-levitation belts puts us in Buck Rogers' 25th Century ahead of time. Within the coming year we will say, *'Look ma I can fly!'*

The threads of *MOM* tech are woven thru the fabric of our lives. Most impressive are health monitors in mirrors, sinks, baths, toilets, jewelry, and cloths. Families, especially children, are now monitored 24/7 with MOM finger rings. Loving thoughts link MOM with loved ones.

MOM lets us focus our thoughts on those we care about. *Oxytocin* is the primary *love-hormone,* assisted by Endorphin, Serotonin, and dopamine.

In mammals and primates, *oxytocin* is produced in the hypothalamus and is stored and secreted by the pituitary. *Oxytocin* and *vasopressin* are the only known hormones released by the posterior pituitary gland to act at a distance.

Oxytocin-neuron links provide amino acid peptides, such as *corticotrophin* and *dynorphin*. These activate brain and brain-stem receptors. *Oxy,* the maternal *bonding* hormone, effects: birth, lactation, wound healing, sex arousal, orgasm, social behavior, pair bonding, and anxiety control.

Oxy promotes group trust empathy. *Oxy* gene faults are linked to sociopath aggression, extending to a propensity toward greed, abuse, violence, and war.

187

Matriarch research continues to explore the organic nature of love and hate. http://en.wikipedia.org/wiki/Oxytocin

Matriarch stewardship is globally accepted. After male leadership gave-up the ghost, what choice was there? Matriarchs ended global violence by means of Global Peace Matrons enforcing conflict resolution. Matrons deal with violence much as with ornery kids. Offenders get work-servitude together with gene therapy.

Pursuit of energy is endless. The frontier is limitless. Mom says, '*Search* is more important than *discovery*.' Mom is fond of repeating Einsteins' quip: '***Getting there is the only home we have.***'

It may be possible to create or use black-holes and orbit these with energy harvester-satellites, such as *Dyson Spheres*. Can we harvest energy from black-holes?

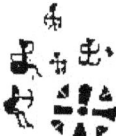

121-Fertility Goddess of birth, moon-crescent archer, and
Cross-shaped sun symbol, Çatalhöyük 6,500 BC

EMag electromagnetism seems like the ideal energy source. It's clean, frictionless, quiet, and limitless. It's like the air and the sun—there for everyone to use, but not abuse.

The Space-Energy lobby is beating the drum about Cosmic Microwave Background Radiation. Now they call it *SpaceN, 'N'* for energy. They say *EMag Earth-magnetics* is the cause of mini-quakes near *EMag* centers.

Mini-quakes occur near old gas fracking wells. *EMag* facilities are licensed to use old fracking and oil wells for tapping into *Earth magnetic* energy. Why drill new wells with all the old wells available?

...*EMag* industries absorb virtually all available workers and still there's a shortage. *EMag* job recycling of millions of workers is the base for building a strong economy and the *MagPak* lobby. Lobbies again, didn't we bury bribery with the entombed leadership?

Matriarchs support beneficial competition; but we can't afford redundant efforts. Now *EMag* seems superior; but conditions change. We need to keep all options open.

SpaceN jobs are hardly a blip on the radar; and it's far more costly than *EMag* due to the need for specialized satellites. The *MagPak* lobby began its own global public relations campaign: 'Will *SpaceN* satellites cause more asteroid storms? Can Mother-Earth survive *SpaceN*?'

There's no solid evidence for these disaster scenarios. *EMag* and *SpaceN* must work together, rather than try to destroy each other. Matrons will finesse cooperation. *SpaceN* uses *HoloVids* of the 2025 California Super-quake for *SpaceN* public relations, PR.

189

EMag PR follows suit with *HoloVids* of the 2026 asteroid-tsunami. Billions died in ten years of disaster.

SpaceN automated their satellites, *sats*, to collect Cosmic Microwave Background Radiation. The *sats* are already laser-beaming CMBR to storage *sats* in orbit and receivers on the Earth, Moon, and Mars.

Georgia Tech has a large grant from *SpaceN* and *EMag* provides Tech with unlimited funds. So far *SpaceN*'s CMBR energy extraction falls short. They've tried to improve their tech for years, with little success. *SpaceN*'s been beating that dead horse for five years. Matrons will negotiate energy peace to limit costs. Competition yes, conflict no.

The 2025 crash made all the difference. Male leaders are gone, destroying their rotten profit-system before they had the decency to self-destruct. Matrons successfully replaced the male wrecking crew. Matrons gently do for the world what they do for their families. Every mother knows her family *works* as long as they have their needs met. Now that all resources are shared, violence is virtually gone.

122-Earth Mother Boetia with cats, 800 BC

Mother's Energy Agency, as in moma-MEA, was the first step in regulating global finance. When private investment was legal again, MEA became the global financial regulator. All financial transactions require a 15% up-front service fee.

While there are *ad hoc* surcharges and service fees, there are no more tax breaks since there are no more taxes. If you start a business, you better plan ahead carefully. Matron advisors provide free counseling. Incentives support growing an enterprise in a socially responsible way. Buy-outs and spin-offs are off the table. Matron Agents monitor and regulate all businesses.

A social safety net now covers the globe, 'from the cradle to the grave'—as they used to say. With instant access to local Matrons, every reasonable need is met. When local matrons need you, best be ready and willing, or lose GEU credits. It's easy to start a small business; but not a big one. Matrons train and guide to advance enterprise success.

Meeting human needs is what family is all about. As mothers are *kinship* family stewards, they are the natural stewards of the *human family*. As stewards of the human family, matriarchs encourage people to be Earth stewards, as well as stewards for each other. Mothers' stewardship includes all families. We are on our way to become one global family. Enough talk; the future is now. Let's get on with it!

19-YEAR 2100:
The year 2100 arrived with less fanfare than expected. Atlanta's infamous traffic jams evaporated as *EMag* power replaced most ground, water, and air traffic. The low altitude skies above Atlanta were getting busy; but with magnetic *repellers* built into all *EMag* transport, it was bumper-cars with gentle *repels* rather than hard *bumps*.

The Atlanta-Montreal Matriarch Republic, AMMR, is an expanse of green reserve stretching to Montreal. The AMMR *Civil Corp* extended the green-belt along the old Appalachian Trail, thru the Adirondacks, and into metro Montreal. The most popular recreation is hiking the AMMR Trail.

123-Winged Sparta Astarte with leopards, 700 BC

The *Corp* serves as a public cooperative, providing a *life-bridge* for people able and willing to learn and work.

Family support systems are global, thanks to local Matron Stewards and *Block Committees*. As substance-control laws disappeared, substance abuse and crime fell. Genetic *GeneMod* with *NanoBot* nasal spray and skin patches eliminates most addictions. Addicts are *persuaded* to enlist in the *Corp,* for care, treatment, education, and service.

All public service is now part of the *Corp*. This includes Matron Stewards, Matron Public Safety, *Block Committees,* transport, sanitation, health, media, and communication. The *Corp* is now the largest employer. The *Corp* is a work-study university for those utilizing the perks. The *Corp* produces its own food, housing, healthcare, and *Corp* people live in family units.

In spring northwest Georgia looks like a white-out. Adding gold, umber, pink, and green hybrids provide rainbow strokes of color to the *Dogwood* Republic.

Most Matriarch Republics adopted the Atlanta-Montreal model of assessing families with above average income a surcharge of from 5% to 90% depending on income.

Pre-collapse problems began with the disastrous accumulation of private wealth, creating global social pathology. This situation is now prohibited. Maximum family income is limited to three times the average. Years ago Huey Long created the *Share Our Wealth* program.
http://en.wikipedia.org/wiki/Huey_Long

124-Mycenaean Astarte in leopard skins 3,500 BC

Matriarchs have implemented many of these ideas. Matriarch Republic funds are gathered in part from surcharges paid into the republic's investment *cloud*. Families with below average income receive family support to bring them up to the average.

Robots fill the labor gap between people and jobs. People are guaranteed employment preference. Robots are used for dangerous, repetitious, and extremely hard work. Fully autonomous systems are prohibited. All automation, including robots, must be initiated, monitored, and terminated by people. We learned this lesson from *drones*.

Nola and Pal were now the ancestors of their own Mik-Sem Clan, numbering in the hundreds. That morning the latest addition Susana-Noel age four hours appeared in all her glory on the Mik-Sem tribal network registry. Every September the Mik-Sem tribe holds its annual *pow-wow* week where new arrivals are presented.

It was Ancestors Day at the Tribal Forum. Nola and Pal were asked to provide the New Century Tribal Address. The Address would be presented live, broadcast, and recorded in *HoloVid* on the Inner Planetary Network. The Mik-Sem audience sprawls around a slowly rotating *MagLev* center stage. Nola begins with a welcome prayer.

'Welcome Mik-Sem! Today we renew the Mik-Sem story of Sky-Mother and her children:
'In the beginning, there is no beginning.
In the end, there is no end.
SKY-MOTHER and HER children are perpetually reborn.
SHE is Cosmos. SHE is energy. SHE is eternal creator.
SHE creates her children and HER children create HER.
SHE is change and change is our only home.
SHE is all that is revealed. SHE is all that is hidden.
SHE hides in plain sight. HER cosmic charms ensnare.
We are home in HER ever changing cosmic womb.
SHE is the object of our search for hidden knowledge.
Blessed be SKY-MOTHER. Blessed be Cosmic-Mother.
Blessed be Mother-Nature.'

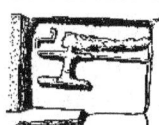

125-Flying Goddess Shrine, Çatalhöyük 6,000 BC

195

'We speculate how energy communicates. It's not magic, just technology not yet understood.
'We want to know *Sky-Mother in all her aspects.*'

'We now measure extremely high and low levels of electromagnetic energy. We track **Dark Energy, Black holes,** and Cosmic Background Microwave Radiation.

'There's a *full plate* of unanswered questions. Consciousness and communication between energy bits are less magical. Thank *Sky-Mother* for the continuing challenge!

'*Quantum entanglement* and instant *worm-hole* communication are speeds of 64 quadrillion miles per second; that's light-speed cubed. This means that all energy communicates with all parts of the Cosmos in fractions of a second, instantly.

'Is *Dark Energy* the 22nd Century *ether*? Does *Dark Energy* provide a cosmic Internet? Keep in mind the old cliché: *If you can imagine it, it will happen.* This lends new meaning to the dream of universal instantaneous communication.

'To see the direction of the future we need to picture where we've been. If we can send brain waves through the Cosmos at virtually instantaneous speed, is this another tech we don't fully understand? Einstein would say: *as the data are incomplete our understanding is incomplete.*

'The Mik-Sem *Sky-Mother* story takes us back to the last cosmic recycling 14-billion years ago.

126 & 127-Spotted Leopard mother, Çatalhöyük 6,500 BC

'At the end of cosmic expansion and cooling, every 14-billion years, a *big-crunch* condenses all weakened cosmic energy into an unstable *singularity*. The singularity expands into a *big-bang* and *big-crunch* again, 14 billion years later. Cosmic recycling is still just a theory.

'Send your imagination back five billion years to the formation of our solar system. Research suggests the formation was violent; beginning with unstable planetary orbits and many collisions.

'A moon of planet X collided with a large watery planet, splitting it. Earth got most of the water. Our moon and Asteroid belt were left with little water.

'Comet, meteor, and Asteroid debris fall to Earth daily. *Panspermia* theory is based on these *visitors*. This *all-seed* theory suggests life exists throughout the Cosmos. Water, methane, carbon dioxide, and amino acids are found in various space explorations. Viable encysted staph bacteria were found on a discarded moon-surface vehicle.

'It took 5-million years from the branching of primates to *Homo erectus*. *Neanderthal* is 1-million years old.

'So how did *modern* humans emerge in only 200,000 years? Digs indicate *Neanderthal*s mated *modern* humans emerging from northeast Africa into the Middle East.'

128-Canaanite Astarte 3,500 BC

'98% of human genes are shared with chimps—except for 250 genes not found in any other species on Earth. If Earth was *terraformed* by collisions, then perhaps we were *human-formed* with the extra 250 genes.

'*Let us create them in our image and after our likeness.* Did *Sky-Mother* create our creators, who in turn created humanity? If we are the *image* and *likeness* of our *creators*, then it's likely we received some of their *intelligence* also.

'With our intelligence we continue to seek *hidden knowledge*. We want to know the *how* and *why* of everything. Much of our pursuit of *hidden knowledge* involves *mating, energy,* and *longevity*.

'I suggest the pursuit of *hidden knowledge* begins with *sexual exploration*. If the gift of sex is genetic, then sexual curiosity is in our genes. Born of mother's *eternal* energy, we seek to return to her great cosmic energy ocean.

'***Sky-mother*** is the *eternal feminine*. SHE is a cosmic ocean of energy. We strive to return to the security, warmth, and nurturing of Sky-Mother's womb.'

129-Çatalhöyük Earth-mother and twin leopards 6,500 BC

'Let's focus attention on the human pursuit of knowledge. Does our search for *hidden knowledge* begin with *sexual curiosity*? Pursuing *knowledge* is a sexual adventure. At first we crave mother; later we crave a mate. Are we searching for a *parent* in each person we encounter? The search is to find a mate, create a family, and teach our kids.

'This is the *mating road*. It is a craving to ***know*** in the Biblical sense. Pursuit of hidden knowledge in science, or sexual exploration, is the *animal magnetism* drawing us closer to the *eternal feminine*.

199

'Sexual intimacy is the goal we seek. Along the *mating road*, we learn, discover, solve problems, and expand the human mind. For these reasons the pursuit of sexual knowledge and the *eternal feminine* create the drive to pursue all *hidden knowledge*.

As there is no Beginning, there is no Ending.
We are home in the process of searching.
Our only home is getting there, not being there.
Blessed be SKY-MOTHER!

20-How to boil a frog: (Based on the *Story of B*, by Daniel Quinn)

Put a frog in a *cauldron* of warm water.
As the water slowly heats, the frog remains still.
The frog goes into a *stupor*, as we might in a *warm bath*.
The frog will *boil* to *death, while* remaining in a *stupor*.
This is a metaphor of the *human condition*.
For 3-million years our ancestors were *hunter-gatherers*.
Modern humans are 200,000 years old.
For 190,000 years we were hunter-gatherers, *Leavers*.
Leavers satisfy daily needs and leave the rest.
Leavers left Africa for the Middle East 50,000 years ago.
The *agricultural revolution* began 10,000 years ago.
The **cauldron** of **humanity** was comfortably warm.
Cataclysmic die-offs occur every 16,000 years or so.
The last die-off was the *great flood* 13,000 years ago.

200

Genesis tells of *Cain the farmer* & *Abel the herder*.
Takers are farmers and herders, as in the American West.
Takers keep grabbing more land, eliminating competitors.
The cauldron was slowly warming.
Farming/herding is harder work than gathering/hunting.
Farmers need field labor and soldiers to guard the land.
More food leads to more people and more land grabbing.
Takers expand without limit, overcoming all opposition.
Amazon deforestation grazes cattle for cheap burgers.
The *cauldron was heating*.
Takers forget the first 190,000 years as **Leavers**.
Takers farm more, but **population** grows faster.
Takers believe in a *God-given right* to take the world.
They take what they want, leaving *eco-disaster*.
Cain-Abel warfare continues where it began.
The cauldron is near *boiling*.
Are we frogs too *stupefied* to *save* ourselves?

The End?

21-Visual sources not previously credited

American School of Classical Studies at Athens, *Miniature Sculpture from the Athenian Agora*, Princeton, 1959

Boardman, John, *Greek Art*, Praeger, NY, 1964

Boas, Franz, *Primitive Art*, Dover, NY, 1955

Fewkes, J. W., *Designs on Prehistoric Hopi Pottery*, Dover, NY, 1973

Gabus, Jean and Roger-Louis Junod, *Amlash Art*, Halwag, Berne, 1967

Hawkes, Jacquetta, *The World of the Past*, Knopf, NY, 1963

Higgins, R., *Minoan and Mycenaean Art*, Praeger, NY, 1967

Kroeber, A. L., *Handbook of Indians of California*, Dover, NY, 1976

Mair, Lucy, *Witchcraft*, McGraw-Hill, NY, 1969

Mellaart, James, *Çatalhöyük*, McGraw-Hill, NY, 1967

_____, *Earliest Civilizations Near East*, McGraw-Hill, NY, 1967

Petrie, Flinders, *Decorative Patterns of Ancient World for Craftsmen*, Dover, NY

Schaafsma, Polly, *Rock Art in the Navajo Reservoir District*, Papers in Anthropology #7, Museum New Mexico Press, Santa Fe, 1971

Schultz, Paul E., *Indians of Lassen Volcanic National Park Vicinity*, Loomis Museum Association, Mineral, CA, 1954

Speck, Frank Gouldsmith, *The Iroquois*, Cranbrook Institute of Science Bloomfield Hills, Michigan, 1955

130-Bull-jumping honors the goddess, Knossos, Crete 1000BC